RECIPE PLEASE

From the popular column in the
Rocky Mountain News

RECPE
PLEASE

Favorite Recipes from Colorado Restaurants

Marty Meitus

Food Editor

Johnson Books
BOULDER, COLORADO

Published by Johnson Books, a division of Johnson Publishing Company, 1880 South 57th Court, Boulder, Colorado 80301.
E-mail: books@jpcolorado.com
www.johnsonbooks.com

9 8 7 6 5 4 3 2

Cover design: Tangram Design
Text design: Eric Christensen

Library of Congress Cataloging-in-Publication Data
Recipe, please: favorite recipes from Colorado restaurants / edited by Marty Meitus.
        p. cm.
    Includes index.
    ISBN 1-55566-332-X
    1. Cookery. 2. Cookery—Colorado. I. Meitus, Marty, 1952–
    TX714.R42216 2004
    641.5—dc22   2004014549

Printed in the United States by
Johnson Printing
1880 South 57th Court
Boulder, Colorado 80301

Printed on ECF paper with soy ink

Contents

Teriyaki Salmon

Serves 4

1 cup soy sauce
Juice of one lemon
¼ cup dry sherry
¼ cup green onions
2 tablespoons minced fresh ginger root
1 garlic clove, minced
1 tablespoon freshly ground pepper
4 salmon fillets

■ Combine the soy sauce, lemon juice, sherry, green onions, ginger root, garlic and pepper in a shallow dish.
■ Add the salmon, turning to coat. Marinate, covered, in the refrigerator for 5 to 8 hours. Drain.
■ Grill the salmon over hot coals for 5 to 7 minutes on each side. — *The Redneck Grill*

Nutritional information per serving:
150 cal., 6 g fat (1 g sat.), 20 mg chol., 4 g carb., 825 mg sodium, 0 fiber, 16 g pro.

Hearts Of Palm Salad

ost
short
ice of food
it.
r, who's British,
what are the odds
d is going to eat
sh Pie: a layer of
atoes hiding a delecta-
n of cod, smoked had-
ed egg and peas? I
lots of brain foods
I'm smart enough
ese recipes will never

ck Grill (Jeff Foxwor-
Hill Press, $15.99). Ap-
xworthy is a barbecuing
which means he gets to
kbook. The subtitle of the
most fun you can have
arcoal and a dead ani-
doesn't put you off—i.e.,
worthy fan — the reci-
ith redneck jokes and
kled about to spice

My thanks to: John Temple and the *Rocky Mountain News*

Special thanks to: Mike Pearson, Denny Dressman, Sue Kramer, and Karen Bellofatto

To those who were invaluable in the testing: Jan Crain Rudeen; Judie and Jeff Schwartz; Robin and Stu Pack; Linny and Roger Pretekin; Nicki and Irv Zwick; Patti Thorn and Harold Dubinski; Laurie and Rob Abramson.

And as always: To Doug, Melissa, and Jacob

Preface

In 1997, the *Rocky Mountain News* launched a column that would bring the restaurants of Colorado into your home kitchen. By way of introduction, I wrote, "Do you want to make crab cakes like your favorite restaurant does? Do you want to enjoy that special restaurant experience at home? Send us your request and we'll arm-wrestle a few chefs for you." Since that time, we have run a recipe from a restaurant every week, and the column, which appears every Saturday in the Home Front section, is still going strong.

The number of requests readers have sent in has been astounding. Surprisingly, people are most interested in obtaining recipes for soups and salad dressings and bread puddings, although we have satisfied requests for everything from salsa to short ribs, from pound cake to pasta. Thus, many of the dishes are comfort food, while others follow the trend du jour.

I had no idea when we undertook this column that I really would be arm-wrestling a chef or two. It's a challenge to persuade a chef to sit down, put pen to paper, and come up with a recipe that will serve 4, or 6, or 8 rather than 40, or 60, or 80. Another challenge was that chefs are notorious for improvising—forgetting to mention that this or that ingredient just happens to be critical to a dish. Jan Crain Rudeen has been invaluable in testing the recipes the first time around, making sense of ingredients and instructions to ensure the recipes can be made at home.

In the few years since the column began, many of the ingredients called for in these recipes, once available primarily to chefs, are showing up in the aisles of mainstream grocery stores, making it easier than ever to "cook like a chef." In this book, we have collected the most memorable and delicious of the dishes our readers have requested. A number of the recipes are easy enough to whip up for breakfast, lunch, or dinner, yet elegant enough for company. The "Eggs Taos" recipe from the Bull and Bush comes to mind, as does the "Penne Mona Lisa" from Bruno's.

Do we have favorites among the group represented here? Most definitely. And we've even had a few surprises. My kids, as it turned out, love the "Pumpkin Chocolate Chip Cookies" from The Market, and my husband has turned out to be a meatloaf fan. If you're looking for a great recipe for chocolate chip cookies, we've got one from Michael Bortz—or, if you want a dessert recipe to wow 'em, we've got those, too, with everything from the "White Chocolate Mousse with Ganache" from Strings to "Apple Crostata" from Maggiano's. And don't let on where you got the fabulous recipe for Sean Kelly's hummus, which I often claim at parties as my own.

Responding to the economic cycles of Colorado, many of the chefs and/or restaurateurs have moved on to other locales or other restaurants. The book is as much a walk down restaurant memory lane as it is a cookbook—a feast of nostalgia as well as a feast for the table. We have done our best to gather enough recipes to give you variety and, in some cases, to allow you to discover your preferred recipe for a particular kind of dish, as with the several butternut squash soups and bread puddings. We hope you'll be tempted to try them all and that many of these will become cherished favorites.

Appetizers & First Courses

Broiled Sea Scallops Wrapped in Bacon with Apricot Chutney   3

Chinese Lettuce Wraps with Shrimp   4

Coconut Shrimp   5

Coconut Shrimp with Orange Horseradish Sauce   6

Shrimp Ceviche   7

Crab Cakes with Remoulade Sauce   8

Lump Crab Cakes   10

Portobello Mushrooms Stuffed with Lobster, Crab, and Goat Cheese   11

Asian-Style Hot Wings   12

Yuppie-I-O Dip   13

Gaucho Dip   14

Spinach-Artichoke Dip   15

Artichoke Dip   16

Wynkoop's Famous Cheesy Artichoke Dip   17

Southwestern Cheese Dip   18

Hummus   19

Roasted Tomato Salsa   20

Lemon Drop Martini   21

Broiled Sea Scallops Wrapped in Bacon with Apricot Chutney

This recipe is a stand-out as a first course, if you really want to impress your guests at a dinner party.

SERVES 8

Preheat oven to 350 degrees.

Cook bacon strips in oven until half done, approximately 13 minutes. Remove bacon from oven and wrap bacon around the circumference of each scallop. Place scallops in buttered dish large enough to fit them comfortably without touching. Brush scallops lightly with melted butter. Broil for 8 minutes or until scallop is cooked through, turning once.

To serve, place chutney in center of platter and arrange spinach leaves on platter, alternating with lemon quarters. Arrange cooked scallops on top of spinach. Serve immediately.

12 slices bacon
12 large sea scallops
8 leaves spinach,
    washed and stems removed
1/2 cup Apricot Chutney
    (see recipe that follows)
2 tablespoons melted butter
2 lemons quartered

Cook's Tip: Lay the scallops flat and wrap the bacon around the circumference of the scallops, the way you would if you were wrapping a piece of bacon around filet mignon.

Apricot Chutney

MAKES 1 1/2 CUPS

In stainless-steel bowl, whip apricot preserves until smooth. Add horseradish and pepper. Blend thoroughly and refrigerate until serving time.

1 cup apricot preserves
1/2 cup horseradish, strained
2 teaspoons freshly cracked pepper

Chinese Lettuce Wraps with Shrimp

Johnny Hsu of the Imperial and Palace Chinese Restaurants makes his lettuce wraps with tender butter lettuce leaves.

SERVES 6 TO 8

Peel and devein shrimp. Mix shrimp with cornstarch in a strainer. Rinse the cornstarch from the shrimp until they look clean. Leave shrimp in strainer to drain excess water.

Cut celery, red bell pepper, mushrooms, and jicama into small dice (about 1/4-inch squares). Trim and clean lettuce leaves.

Pour oil into a heated wok. Add shrimp and stir-fry until they turn pink. Add other chopped vegetables, and keep stir-frying until the aroma rises; then pour in the All-Flavor Sauce. Bring to a boil; add pine nuts. Divide shrimp mixture evenly by spooning into individual lettuce leaves. Fold leaf ends around filling to create a wrap and serve.

All-Flavor Sauce

MAKES 1/2 CUP

Put all ingredients in a bowl and mix well.

1 pound raw small shrimp
2 tablespoons cornstarch
1 stalk celery
1/2 red bell pepper, seeded
16 fresh button mushrooms, washed and patted dry
3 ounces jicama, peeled
8 Bibb lettuce leaves
1 tablespoon vegetable oil
2 tablespoons pine nuts
All-Flavor Sauce (see recipe that follows)

3 teaspoons soy sauce
1 teaspoon Kitchen Bouquet or Maggi seasoning
5 teaspoons ketchup
3 teaspoons sugar
2 teaspoons red or plum vinegar
2 teaspoons sake
2 teaspoons sesame oil

. . . .

Coconut Shrimp

Coconut shrimp is a popular request. A Denver classic, Racines enjoyed almost twenty years of popularity in its old location and will no doubt enjoy the same popularity at its new location a few blocks away.

SERVES 6 TO 8

Peel shrimp, leaving the tail attached. Devein shrimp and rinse with cold water. Dust lightly with flour. Dip in egg wash. Dredge in flaked coconut. Deep-fry in oil at 350 degrees approximately 4 to 5 minutes until golden brown. You may also stir-fry the shrimp, which works equally well. Place shrimp on warm platter, garnish with almonds, and serve with dipping sauce.

36 large raw shrimp (approximately)
Flour
Egg wash (1 part egg to 1 part water)
Sweetened flaked coconut
Vegetable oil for deep-frying
Sour Cream–Curry Dipping Sauce
   (see recipe that follows)
Toasted sliced almonds for garnish

Sour Cream–Curry Dipping Sauce

MAKES 1 1/2 CUPS

Melt butter in small saucepan. Sauté apples and onion in butter until soft. Add curry powder and blend well. Add chicken stock and reduce liquid by half. In blender, puree mixture until smooth and cool. Chill until cool enough to add sour cream without curdling it. Add sour cream to chilled mixture and blend.

3 tablespoons butter
2 apples, peeled, cored, and diced
1/2 onion, finely diced
2 tablespoons curry powder
1 1/2 cups chicken stock
1 cup sour cream

. . . .

Coconut Shrimp with Orange Horseradish Sauce

This tasty dish started as an appetizer at the Wellshire Inn as part of a four-course special. It proved so popular that diners began asking for it—without the special.

SERVES 4 TO 6

Butterfly shrimp. Mix coconut and bread crumbs together and season with salt and pepper.

Beat eggs with water. Dip shrimp into egg mixture, then coconut. Deep-fry at 375 degrees for 2 to 3 minutes until golden brown.

Place shrimp in a warmed dish or plate and serve with sauce. Garnish with chives.

Cook's Tip: To butterfly shrimp, cut along the front of the shrimp as if you were going to cut in half, but don't cut all the way through. The halves should lie flat the way they would if you were opening a book.

4 raw jumbo shrimp per person
1 cup sweetened flaked coconut
1 cup panko or Asian-style bread crumbs (available at Asian markets or the Asian food aisles of most grocery stores)
1 teaspoon salt
1 teaspoon pepper
6 eggs
1/2 cup water
Vegetable oil for deep-frying
Orange Horseradish Sauce (see recipe that follows)
Chopped chives for garnish

Orange Horseradish Sauce

MAKES 1²/₃ CUPS

Puree all ingredients in blender until smooth.

1 cup sun-dried apricots
1 cup orange marmalade
1/4 cup fresh orange juice
2 tablespoons fresh lime juice
1/3 cup plus 2 teaspoons prepared horseradish

Shrimp Ceviche

Ceviche is usually made with scallops that are marinated or "cooked" overnight in lime juice. This version from Seven 30 South avoids the issue of uncooked seafood by substituting cooked rock shrimp for the scallops.

SERVES 6

Cook the rock shrimp in boiling salted water. Drain and cool. Dice the tomatoes and onion to a medium dice. Chop the cilantro fine and mix with the tomatoes and onions. Squeeze the juice of the limes into the cilantro and tomato mixture. Add the shrimp, salt and pepper, and toss to combine.

1 pound raw rock shrimp
6 ripe tomatoes
1 yellow onion
1 bunch fresh cilantro
3 limes
1 teaspoon salt
1 teaspoon ground pepper

Cook's Tip: Rock shrimp, named for their rock-hard shells, have gained in popularity in the last few years. Their texture is somewhat like lobster, with a taste more like shrimp. You will need to order them from your butcher at the supermarket or look for them at specialty grocery stores.

Crab Cakes with Remoulade Sauce

These are delicious, but they do take time to prepare. Because there is no binder other than the cream, you'll have to really press the crab cakes together with your hands or they'll fall apart when frying. I chopped the bell peppers and onion in a food processor so I'd have really small pieces.

MAKES ABOUT 10, DEPENDING ON SIZE

Place cream, jalapeño, and cayenne in a saucepan over medium heat. (Do not cut the jalapeño.) Reduce by half. Strain the cream through a small sieve; cool.

Place the bell peppers and the onion in a sauté pan, over medium heat, and cook, covered, until softened and any accumulated juices have evaporated.

Wring out excess water in the crab meat by wrapping in a clean dish towel and squeezing. Fold together the crab meat, the strained cream, the pepper-onion mixture, and the herbs.

1 cup heavy whipping cream
1 jalapeño pepper
$1/8$ teaspoon cayenne pepper
$1/2$ red bell pepper, finely diced
$1/2$ green bell pepper, finely diced
$1/2$ yellow onion, finely diced
1 pound fresh crab meat, or frozen, thawed
2 tablespoons chopped parsley (optional)
$1^{1}/2$ tablespoons chopped fresh thyme
Flour
1 egg, combined with 2 tablespoons water
Bread crumbs
Vegetable oil for frying
Remoulade Sauce (see recipe that follows)

Form crab meat mixture into patties. Dip in flour, then egg wash, then bread crumbs.

Heat oil in pan. You may deep-fry, keeping the temperature at 325 degrees, or panfry in about $1/4$-inch vegetable oil until crab cakes are crispy on the outside and cooked inside— about 8 minutes total, turning once.

Serve with Remoulade Sauce.

Remoulade Sauce

MAKES 1^{1}/$_{4}$ CUPS

Mix all ingredients together. Taste and adjust seasonings.

1 cup mayonnaise
2 tablespoons ketchup
1 tablespoon Dijon mustard
^{1}/$_{2}$ red onion, minced
^{1}/$_{2}$ dill pickle, finely diced
^{1}/$_{8}$ cup capers
Fresh dill, chopped, to taste
^{1}/$_{8}$ teaspoon cayenne
^{1}/$_{8}$ teaspoon paprika
Juice of ^{1}/$_{4}$ lemon

Lump Crab Cakes

This dish was a huge hit with company—as are all of chef/owner Patricia Perry's recipes. But be forewarned that crab cakes are an art unto themselves. The secret is to use only as much mayonnaise as needed to keep them from falling apart, and to make them small enough to turn easily. After a friend watched me struggle to turn them intact, she went out and bought me a mini-spatula, which made the process a whole lot easier.

SERVES 6 TO 8

Put crab meat in a large mixing bowl. In a smaller bowl, mix together mayo, mustard powder, parsley, chives, and red bell pepper; blend thoroughly. Add lemon juice, salt, and pepper, adjusting for taste. Gently fold this mixture into the crab meat in order to retain the crab meat's dense lumps of flesh.

Form crab mixture into balls using the palms of your hands. If the crab meat doesn't hold together, add more mayonnaise and blend.

Pour bread crumbs onto a plate and whisk in the garlic powder. Gently roll each crab meat ball in the seasoned crumbs and flatten each a bit to form a cake. Try not to make cakes too big.

2 pounds lump blue crab, picked through and checked for bits of shell; or the equivalent in canned crab
2 tablespoons mayonnaise (start with this amount, but increase as needed)
2 teaspoons Coleman's dry mustard
2 tablespoons chopped Italian parsley
2 tablespoons chopped chives or scallions
2 tablespoons red bell pepper, finely diced
Juice of 1 lemon
2 pinches of salt
2 pinches of coarsely ground pepper
1 cup bread crumbs
$1/2$ teaspoon garlic powder
1 to 2 tablespoons olive oil
Lemon slices for garnish

Heat the oil on a griddle or in a heavy frying pan over medium-high heat. Carefully place crab cakes in the pan and brown on each side, turning gently. If crab cakes fall apart, try to push back together with the spatula. Place browned crab cakes in a baking dish or on a cookie sheet and finish in a 350-degree oven for about 5 minutes.

Serve with favorite cocktail sauce or Remoulade Sauce (see recipe on p. 9) and lemon slices.

Portobello Mushrooms Stuffed with Lobster, Crab, and Goat Cheese

Cade Nagy bought Paul's Catering a few years ago. An offshoot of Paul's Place, which was known for its hot dogs and hamburgers, Nagy has taken it to the next level of catering with upscale and tasty items. This mushroom dish was the hit of one of the "Taste of Colorado" festivals.

SERVES 3 TO 6

3 large or 12 smaller-sized
   portobello mushrooms
$1/2$ cup salad oil
$1/4$ cup balsamic vinegar
Salt and pepper to taste
Meat from 1 lobster tail, cooked and diced
   ($1/2$ pound)
$6^1/2$ ounces lump crab meat
4 ounces goat cheese
2 ounces cream cheese
1 tablespoon chopped parsley
1 clove garlic, crushed
Fresh chives for garnish

Trim the mushroom stems to $1/2$ inch. Dip the mushroom caps in oil and set them on the grill. Drizzle oil and vinegar over the stem side and season with salt and pepper. Cook them as you would a burger, to desired doneness, turning them once. (You can also broil. Mushrooms will take 3 to 5 minutes per side.) Set mushrooms aside, stem side up, on a sheet pan.

In a medium mixing bowl, toss remaining ingredients, except chives, and mix well. Let soften, about 1 hour. Using a pastry bag, pipe mixture equally on the mushrooms or spoon on mixture with a tablespoon if you prefer not to pipe. Place pan in oven preheated to 350 degrees and heat until cheese is hot and warmed through. Serve on a platter with your favorite butter sauce, such as hollandaise, or with just lemon wedges. Garnish with fresh chives.

Note: Recipe may be doubled.

Asian-Style Hot Wings

Ray Flores, owner of Big Ray's Chop House, gives an Asian flair to the traditional buffalo wings.

SERVES 8

Preheat oven to 375 degrees.

Bake chicken wings for 45 minutes or until cooked through. (You may also broil or deep-fry them.) Remove chicken from the pan and place in a large bowl. Pour sauce over wings, tossing wings until well coated. Serve with ranch or blue cheese dressing.

Asian Hot Wing Sauce

MAKES 2 CUPS

Combine all ingredients and mix well.

4 pounds chicken wings
Asian Hot Wing Sauce
   (see recipe that follows)
Ranch dressing or blue cheese dressing,
   for dipping (optional)

Cook's Tip: Sriacha sauce is a Thai chili sauce, commonly found in plastic squeeze bottles on tables in Thai restaurants. Flores uses the Tuong Ot brand of sriacha. He also deep-fries the wings, but I baked them instead.

1/2 cup sriacha sauce (in the Asian section
   of most groceries or at Asian markets)
1/8 cup honey
1 tablespoon melted butter
1 1/2 cups soy sauce

Yuppie-I-O Dip

Castle Café is always busy, serving up its famous fried chicken and sides, but the Yuppie-I-O spinach and artichoke dip is an absolutely delicious way to start the meal.

SERVES 10 TO 12

Blend cream cheese in food processor until smooth. Remove from processor and mix in a bowl with all remaining ingredients. Place in shallow, broiler-proof casserole dish and broil until golden on top.

Cook's Tip: When a friend of mine made this for a dinner party, she couldn't decide whether or not to puree all the ingredients in the food processor, so she tried it both ways. When she pureed everything, it turned a bright green color not usually found in food, but some people didn't mind the color and preferred the smoother texture. I prefer my dips a little chunkier—the way it's served at the restaurant—so I mix, not puree, the ingredients.

$^1/_2$ pound cream cheese, softened
1$^1/_2$ cups grated Parmesan
1$^1/_2$ cups mayonnaise
7 ounces artichoke hearts, drained, chopped
$^1/_4$ pound fresh spinach, washed, patted dry, and chopped
$^1/_4$ small yellow onion, julienned

Gaucho Dip

When dipping bread in an oil and balsamic vinegar dip became the hit of restaurants, the Wellshire Inn came up with its own version: the Gaucho Dip. It would also make a great dressing for a cold pasta salad.

MAKES 5 CUPS

Wash and dry all herbs thoroughly. Place all ingredients in blender and pulse, making sure you do not liquefy the herbs. Serve as a dip for a rustic-style bread with crispy crust or use as a dressing for pasta salad.

3/4 bunch parsley
3/4 bunch cilantro
1 tablespoon fresh mint
1/4 cup fresh basil
2 cloves garlic
1 teaspoon crushed red pepper
1 teaspoon kosher salt
1/2 teaspoon fresh lemon juice
3 tablespoons red wine vinegar
1 quart olive oil

. . . .

Spinach-Artichoke Dip

Chefs have been adding their own spin to the classic cream cheese and artichoke dip ever since it replaced California onion dip as a party favorite. You'll find a number of variations on this theme, including this popular update. I'd be hard-pressed to name which one is my favorite.

SERVES 12

Prepare spinach according to package directions; allow cooked spinach to cool. Meanwhile, chop the artichoke hearts and mix with remaining ingredients.

When spinach is cool enough to handle, squeeze out excess liquid; then add the spinach to the cream cheese mixture and stir until blended. After mixing, adjust seasonings, such as seasoned salt and celery salt to taste. Place mixture in an ovenproof dish and warm in oven at 300 degrees until just heated through.

Serve with pita chips and celery and carrot sticks.

Note: Recipe can be doubled.

1 1/2 pounds frozen chopped spinach
1 small can (about 5 count) artichoke hearts
1 1/2 pounds cream cheese, softened
2 green onions, finely sliced
1 1/2 cloves garlic, minced
1 tablespoon chopped fresh dill weed
1 tablespoon celery salt
1 teaspoon white pepper
1 1/2 teaspoons seasoned salt
1 cup sour cream
1/2 cup shredded Parmesan
1/4 cup white wine

. . . .

Artichoke Dip

We've tried many artichoke dips, including the standard green chile and mayo, but this one was a delicious surprise. As one person said, "It has a lot more zip than the others."

SERVES 8

Preheat oven to 375 degrees.

Using a mixer, blend all ingredients well. Place into shallow, ovenproof bowls or serving pans and bake for 45 minutes or until top is brown. If you are in a hurry, you can microwave for 60 seconds per pound, then bake in the oven at 375 degrees for 10 minutes. Let stand for 10 minutes to cool slightly.

Cook's Tip: I've seen the garlic called for in this recipe as either granular or granulated. Either way, you'll find it in the spice aisles at the grocery stores. (Be sure you don't substitute garlic salt instead—it'll make the dip far too salty.) The granules provide the flavor of garlic when you don't want a mouthful of garlic pieces in a dish.

2 8-ounce packages cream cheese, softened
$1/2$ cup mayonnaise
1 cup grated Parmesan
1 tablespoon granulated garlic
1 tablespoon white pepper
1 tablespoon chopped fresh dill weed
Salt to taste
2 14-ounce cans artichoke hearts, drained, not marinated

Wynkoop's Famous Cheesy Artichoke Dip

This is a delicious dip. A friend of mine who tried it mixed the whole thing in a food processor, which resulted in a smoother dip. If you want a dip with pieces of artichokes in it, chop the artichokes and mix the ingredients by hand.

SERVES 8 TO 10

Mince white and green parts of green onion. Combine all ingredients and mix well with whisk until thoroughly combined. Heat in a 375-degree oven until mixture is hot to the touch, about 30 minutes. As an alternate cooking method, heat in microwave on high for 3 to 4 minutes until hot, stopping at 30-second intervals to stir.

$1/2$ bunch green onions
1 14-ounce can artichoke hearts, drained and chopped
1 clove fresh garlic, minced
Pinch of ground white pepper
$1/2$ teaspoon celery salt
1 cup sour cream
1 cup mayonnaise
$1/3$ cup grated Parmesan

Southwestern Cheese Dip

Wow, do people love warm, bubbly cheese dips—and with so many to choose from in this book, you can escape the monotony of serving the same one over and over. Racines has always been one of our most popular places for recipe requests.

SERVES 12

Add mayonnaise and sour cream to softened cream cheese. Mix well. Add remaining ingredients except Cheddar and avocado. Mix well. Fold in grated Cheddar.

Place mixture in glass baking dish or divide into smaller portions and spoon into ramekins. Place in oven at 350 degrees for approximately 10 minutes until bubbly and a little brown.

Garnish with sliced avocado and serve with your favorite salsa and warm corn tortilla chips.

$1/2$ cup mayonnaise
$3/4$ cup sour cream
1 pound 4 ounces cream cheese, softened
$1/2$ cup grated Parmesan
1 jalapeño, seeded, finely diced
2 green onions, finely chopped
$1/2$ red bell pepper, seeded and finely chopped
2 6-ounce cans diced green chiles
Pinch of salt
2 teaspoons ground cumin
2 teaspoons chili powder
1 cup grated Cheddar
1 avocado, sliced, for garnish

Hummus

This recipe is one of my personal favorites (which I have made over and over, saying to others, "Well, you think you have a great recipe, wait until you taste mine."). "Mine" is actually a recipe from Sean Kelly, who now presides over the restaurant Clair de Lune. Serve the hummus with pita bread, cut in wedges.

SERVES 8

Strain liquid from garbanzo beans, reserving liquid for recipe. Combine all ingredients in a food processor. Puree to a smooth paste, adding garbanzo bean liquid and other seasonings to achieve desired consistency and flavor. Consistency should be that of a thick dip.

Cook's Tip: Tahini is made of sesame seeds ground to a paste and is usually found next to the peanut butter in mainstream grocery stores— maybe because it looks like peanut butter. It's expensive and comes in a large jar, which is unfortunate because it has a short shelf life. Refrigerate the jar after opening.

2 15-ounce cans garbanzo beans
  (also known as chickpeas)
2 to 3 garlic cloves
1/2 cup packed cilantro leaves
1 1/2 tablespoons tahini
1/4 cup fresh lemon juice
1/3 cup olive oil
1/2 to 3/4 cup liquid from canned beans
Salt to taste

Roasted Tomato Salsa

Mexicali in LoDo closed a few years ago, but it was owned by the Larimer Group, which has Josephina's, so the recipe was still available. Note that this is a roasted tomato salsa with cumin as the secret ingredient.

MAKES 1 BOWL OF SALSA

Slice tomatoes in half lengthwise and seed each half. Place tomatoes cut-side down on baking sheet and broil for about 5 minutes until roasted and charred.

Put roasted tomatoes in a food processor bowl; pulse a couple times to chop—tomatoes should still be chunky. Place chopped tomatoes in a medium bowl and add the serranos, onion, and cilantro; stir until blended. Mix in remaining spices. Taste to adjust seasonings to suit your preferences and chill salsa before serving.

6 ripe Roma tomatoes
2 to 3 serrano peppers, seeded and diced
1/2 small yellow onion, finely diced
   (or more, if desired)
2 tablespoons chopped fresh cilantro
   (or more to taste)
1 teaspoon ground cumin
Kosher salt to taste
Red pepper chili flakes
   (optional: add if you want hotter salsa)

Cook's Tip: Don't overprocess the roasted tomatoes or you'll end up with tomato puree instead of salsa. This is a good basic salsa. You could modify this by adding lime juice, black beans, and corn or whatever else strikes your fancy.

Lemon Drop Martini

We don't get a lot of requests for alcoholic drinks, but this one is a little different and seemed to suggest spring and summertime. By the way, it's shaken, not stirred.

Smash the lemon wedges in the bottom of a shaker (the bartender uses a tool called a "muddler"). Add the sugar, sweet and sour, Absolut, and ice. Shake. (You may want to taste and adjust flavors—this is supposed to be a drink with a tart taste.) Rim a chilled martini glass with sugar. Strain the mixture into the glass and serve.

Per drink:
2 lemon wedges
$1/2$ teaspoon sugar
Splash of sweet-and-sour (nonalcoholic mixture, available at liquor stores)
$1^1/2$ ounces Absolut Citron
Crushed ice
Sugar for rim of glass

Soups, Chowders, & Stews

(continued on next page)

Soups, Chowders, & Stews, *continued*

Gorgonzola Ale Soup

Beer cheese soups are always at the top of our list of requests. This one is from Denver Mayor John Hickenlooper's restaurant. You can make it with other cheeses—we tried smoked Gouda and it was delicious and easy.

SERVES 6 to 8

Boil potatoes and onion in water until potatoes get slightly mushy, 15 to 20 minutes. Drain water into a bowl and set aside. Puree onion and potatoes in a food processor, adding reserved potato water as needed to make a smooth mixture. Be careful not to splatter because the mixture will be hot.

Meanwhile, pour chicken stock and beer into large stockpot and bring to a boil on the stove. Add the cheese and stir over medium heat until cheese melts and blends. Add cream, pureed potato mixture, salt, and pepper and simmer about 10 minutes. Dissolve cornstarch in the reserved potato water and stir into the soup. Simmer for another 10 minutes and serve steaming hot. Garnish with croutons.

1 pound red potatoes, peeled and chopped
1 medium yellow onion, peeled and chopped
3 quarts water
2 cups chicken stock
$1^1/_2$ cups beer, such as Railyard Ale
$1/_2$ pound Gorgonzola, processed pepperjack, or smoked Gouda
1 cup heavy cream
1 teaspoon salt or to taste
1 teaspoon white pepper or to taste
$1/_4$ cup cornstarch
$1/_2$ cup reserved potato water
Croutons for garnish

Wild Mushroom Bisque with Sherry

This is an absolutely delicious soup. Chef/co-owner Matt Franklin of 240 Union suggests the more wild mushrooms, the better. I used about a half pound of portobello, shiitake, and brown mushrooms and a half pound of white button mushrooms.

1 pound assorted mushrooms, such as shiitake, cremini, portobello, morel, or white mushrooms. (Dried wild mushrooms can also be used. Soak in 2 cups hot water for 3 minutes, but use only 1/2-pound wild and 1/2-pound white mushrooms and use the mushroom water in place of half the stock.)
1 stick butter (1/4 pound or 1/2 cup)
1 medium onion, chopped
6 tablespoons flour
1 teaspoon Worcestershire sauce
1 tablespoon balsamic vinegar
1/4 cup cream sherry
1 quart homemade chicken stock or canned chicken broth
2 cups heavy cream
2 cups milk
Salt and freshly ground pepper to taste

SERVES 10

Wash mushrooms and discard any tough stems. Pat dry and chop all mushrooms together until very fine.

In a large soup kettle, melt butter. Add onion and sauté until lightly browned. Add mushrooms and cook 10 to 12 minutes over medium heat. Add flour to mushroom mixture, stirring over medium heat about 5 minutes. Then add Worcestershire, balsamic vinegar, and half of the sherry and cook 3 to 4 minutes longer. Add stock and simmer 30 minutes; then add cream and milk, bring to a low boil, and simmer another 15 minutes.

Ladle soup into blender in small batches and puree until smooth; during the process, pour pureed batches into a large bowl, preferably with a pouring spout. (If you prefer a chunkier soup, omit blending.) Return soup to soup kettle and stir in remaining sherry and salt and pepper to taste.

Cook's Tip: Portobellos are just the grown-up version of cremini, the small brown mushroom.

⋯⋯⋯⋯⋯⋯⋯⋯⋯⋯⋯⋯⋯⋯⋯⋯⋯⋯⋯⋯⋯⋯⋯⋯⋯⋯⋯⋯

Cream of Mushroom Soup

Although Bella Ristorante has closed, we had numerous requests for their dishes through the years. Use a good quality beef stock to enhance this rich soup.

SERVES 4 TO 6

Heat olive oil in a medium-sized pot. Add onions, fresh basil, garlic, and mushrooms to hot oil and sauté lightly.

Add red wine. When absorbed, add Worcestershire and beef stock and bring to a boil (about 30 seconds).

Add heavy whipping cream and reduce to desired thickness. (Soup should coat the back of a spoon.)

Season with salt and pepper to taste.

Garnish with additional chopped fresh basil.

1 tablespoon olive oil
$1/4$ cup chopped red onions
8 fresh basil leaves, chopped
  (plus additional for garnish)
2 tablespoons chopped garlic
10 jumbo mushrooms, washed,
  patted dry, and sliced
2 tablespoons red wine
2 tablespoons Worcestershire sauce
$1/2$ cup beef stock
4 cups heavy whipping cream
Salt and pepper to taste

Wolfgang Puck's Grand Café Butternut Squash Soup

This recipe is one of Restaurateur Puck's signature dishes. Note that the vegetables in the soup are slow-cooked in the beginning, a procedure that will take about an hour. Also note that it calls for vegetable stock instead of chicken stock.

This recipe is reprinted with the kind permission of Wolfgang Puck, who retains all rights to it.

SERVES 4 TO 6

In a large, heavy pot (at least 5-quart size), melt the butter on low heat. Add the onion, squash, potatoes, and carrots; cover and cook on low heat, stirring occasionally, until vegetables are translucent but not brown, about 1 hour. The objective is to bring out the natural sugars.

Add the vegetable stock, cover, and simmer gently for 2 hours, until the vegetables are soft. Add the cream and curry powder. Transfer to a blender, or use a hand-blender and puree until smooth. Season with salt and white pepper. If needed, adjust sweetness and acidity with the lemon juice and brown sugar.

$1/2$ stick butter (2 ounces or $1/4$ cup)
$1/2$ cup roughly chopped white onion
1 large butternut squash (about 2 to $2^1/2$ pounds), peeled, seeded, and diced
$1^1/4$ pounds potatoes (4 or 5 medium potatoes), peeled and diced
3 large carrots, peeled and diced
1 quart vegetable stock
1 pint cream
2 teaspoons curry powder
Salt and white pepper to taste
2 teaspoons fresh lemon juice (optional)
2 tablespoons brown sugar (optional)

Butternut Squash Soup

Well-known restaurateur Pierre Wolfe had a number of successful restaurants. The Normandy was one of them and the butternut squash soup was one of its most popular dishes. Wolfe still can be heard on the radio with a travel and dining show Sunday afternoons on 1060 A M.

SERVES 8 TO 10

Preheat oven to 350 degrees.

Halve the butternut squashes, scoop out seeds, and place cut-side down in a 9 × 13-inch baking pan; pour about 1 cup of water around the squash. Roast for 45 minutes or until soft. Remove squash from the oven and let cool for 10 minutes. Scoop the flesh away from the peel with a large spoon and reserve. In a large saucepan over medium heat, place the butter, bacon (optional), and onion. Sauté for 6 to 8 minutes. Do not drain. Add dry sherry and sherry vinegar and cook for 2 minutes.

2 butternut squashes
2 tablespoons butter
2 ounces bacon, diced (optional)
1 large onion, diced
3/4 cup dry sherry
2 tablespoons sherry vinegar (optional)
2 potatoes, peeled, diced and
    reserved in cold water
2 quarts chicken stock or broth
2 tablespoons honey
1/2 teaspoon ground cinnamon
1/4 teaspoon ground nutmeg
1/4 teaspoon ground cardamom
1 quart whipping cream
Salt and pepper to taste

Add squash, potatoes, stock, honey, and spices. Simmer for 30 minutes. Remove from heat and puree until smooth. Return to pan and add the whipping cream. Simmer over low heat for 10 minutes and season with salt and pepper.

Note: Recipe can be halved.

Squash Bisque with Wild Rice

Rocky Mountain Diner doesn't confine itself just to panfried chicken and mashed potatoes. You'll find a lot more on its delicious menu, including Summer Squash Bisque with Wild Rice.

SERVES 4

Toss zucchini, yellow squash, onion, garlic, and bell pepper in olive oil with salt and white pepper.

Heat skillet and sauté squash mixture until tender. Transfer to a baking sheet and broil in oven to roast mixture. You will have to watch closely to avoid burning. When a golden brown color is achieved, remove the baking sheet from the oven and transfer half of squash mixture to a blender, and add $1/2$ teaspoon of thyme, $1/2$ teaspoon of basil, and 1 cup chicken stock. Puree and pour into mixing bowl. Repeat with the remaining squash mixture, thyme, basil, and stock. In a $1^1/2$-quart saucepan, heat cream over medium heat; then add pureed mixture and heat thoroughly.

2 zucchini, cut into $1/4$-inch slices
2 yellow squash, cut into $1/4$-inch slices
1 medium onion, cut into $1/4$-inch slices
1 tablespoon minced garlic
1 green bell pepper, stemmed, seeded, and chopped
$1/4$ cup olive oil
Salt and white pepper to taste
1 teaspoon dried thyme
1 teaspoon dried basil
2 cups chicken stock
1 cup heavy cream
Fresh lemon juice to taste
Wild Rice (see recipe that follows)

Season to taste with lemon juice and additional salt and white pepper.

To serve, ladle soup into bowls and place a spoonful of Wild Rice in center.

Wild Rice

MAKES 1 CUP

In a large saucepan, sauté onion in butter. Add sun-dried tomato, water, and wild rice and prepare according to package directions. Stir in parsley at end of cooking time.

1 tablespoon minced onion
1 tablespoon butter
^{1}/$_2$ cup julienned sun-dried tomato
2 cups water
^{1}/$_2$ cup wild rice
Fresh parsley for garnish

. . . .

Tomato Basil Soup

Another winning recipe from California Café, whose recipes have always been among our most requested. Tomato and basil are an irresistible combination. This soup is outstanding.

SERVES 12

In heavy-bottomed stockpot, melt butter and sauté shallots until translucent. Add garlic and sauté 1 minute. Deglaze with white wine. Add canned tomatoes, Roma tomatoes, tomato juice, bay leaves, sugar, baking soda, salt, and pepper. Cook on low heat for 40 minutes or until Roma tomatoes are tender. Add heavy cream and cook for 15 to 20 minutes more. Remove bay leaves. Make a slurry of cornstarch and cold water (shake in a jar). Add to soup, turning up heat and stirring constantly for 1 to 2 minutes until thickened. Do not boil. Remove from heat and stir in basil chiffonade.

Cook's Tip: *To chiffonade the basil, roll the leaves tightly as if you were rolling a cigar, then cut it on the diagonal into thin strips.*

$^1/_2$ stick unsalted butter
   (2 ounces or $^1/_4$ cup)
$^1/_2$ cup finely chopped shallots
$^1/_8$ cup finely chopped garlic
1 cup white wine
3 pounds canned diced tomatoes with juice
$2^1/_2$ pounds fresh Roma tomatoes, diced
2 cups tomato juice
3 bay leaves
$^1/_8$ cup sugar
$^1/_2$ teaspoon baking soda
Salt and pepper to taste
2 quarts heavy cream
$^1/_8$ cup cornstarch
$^1/_2$ cup water
1 cup chiffonade of fresh basil
   (see Cook's Tip that follows)

Note: *Recipe can be halved.*

. . . .

Soups, Chowders, & Stews

32

Tomato Parmesan Soup

Owner Paul Turley has given us this superb soup. If you're a vegetarian who eats dairy products, note that this calls for vegetable stock. Chicken stock is okay, too. Although it's served lukewarm to hot, the soup is light enough for a summertime meal, especially on a rainy day.

SERVES 10 TO 12

In a large soup kettle, melt the butter. Sauté the onions, rosemary, and pepper. Add flour, vegetable stock, and Maggi seasoning. Whisk until smooth. Bring to a boil. Add diced tomatoes. Return to a boil. Add Parmesan and whipping cream. Remove from heat. Stir.

1 stick butter ($1/4$ pound or $1/2$ cup)
$1/2$ cup diced yellow onion
$1/8$ teaspoon rosemary
$1/2$ teaspoon pepper
$3/4$ cup flour
4 cups vegetable stock (canned is fine)
$1/8$ cup Maggi seasoning
2 32-ounce cans diced tomatoes
$1/2$ cup grated Parmesan
2 cups whipping cream

Cook's Note: Maggi is a liquid seasoning that comes in a bottle in the spice aisles of the grocery store.

. . . .

Tomato Bisque with Corn and Fresh Dill

Bump & Grind is a funky spot for breakfast, brunch, and lunch—but there's nothing funky about the quality of the food. (Chef Cliff Trubowitz had the recipe for his Emma Peel cookies appear in *Bon Appetit.*) This honey of a recipe involves two quick steps: sautéing the vegetables and then putting everything in the pot and heating. What could be easier?

SERVES 8

Sauté onion, dill, oregano, and parsley in butter or oil until onion is soft. Add tomatoes and chicken stock; heat.

Add the rest of the ingredients and heat until corn is cooked (about 2 minutes).

1 onion, chopped
2 teaspoons chopped fresh dill
1 1/2 teaspoons fresh oregano
1/4 cup chopped fresh parsley
1/4 cup butter or vegetable oil
3 14-ounce cans chopped tomatoes
4 cups chicken stock
2 teaspoons salt
1/3 cup honey
1 pint half-and-half or whipping cream
1/2 to 2 cups frozen or fresh corn,
  depending on your preference

Cook's Tip: This recipe was tested with half-and-half, but cream would be delicious should you really want to indulge.

. . . .

Roasted Eggplant and Tomato Soup

Bradford Heap, chef/owner of Chautauqua Dining Hall, keeps the restaurant open all year for gracious dining in an elegant setting. Chautauqua was established more than 100 years ago to host cultural events. Dine on the wide verandas of the restaurant in summer or winter and imagine turn-of-the-century folks strolling the grounds with wide-brimmed hats and parasols.

SERVES 8 TO 10

Preheat oven to 350 degrees.

Wash vegetables, pat dry, and brush with canola oil. Place all but red peppers in a shallow baking pan (such as a jelly-roll pan), a large cookie sheet with sides, or on an oven rack covered in foil. Roast for approximately 45 minutes or until tender; watch carefully and do not allow to burn.

Remove vegetables from oven. Next, char red bell peppers under the broiler. It will take about 9 minutes to blacken skin, turning every

5 medium eggplants
3 large ripe tomatoes
3 sweet onions
3 red bell peppers
2 medium carrots, quartered
Canola oil (or other vegetable oil)
2 quarts cold water
1/4 cup chopped garlic cloves
1/4 cup chopped fresh basil leaves
4 sprigs fresh thyme
1 bay leaf
Kosher salt to taste
Freshly ground pepper to taste
Extra-virgin olive oil for garnish

3 minutes with tongs. Place charred peppers in a bowl and cover with plastic wrap, allowing them to "sweat." Peel, cut open, and remove seeds and membranes.

Core the tomatoes when cool. Cut eggplants in half lengthwise and scoop out flesh with a large spoon. Discard purple skins.

(continued on next page)

Put all roasted vegetables in a stockpot and add 2 quarts cold water. Tie herbs into a small piece of cheesecloth like a sachet and place in pot (this flavoring packet is also referred to as a bouquet garni). Bring to a simmer and cook over low heat for 30 minutes. Cool.

Remove herbs. Puree vegetables in batches in blender or food processor until smooth.

Reheat and season to taste with kosher salt and freshly ground pepper. Serve in soup bowls with a drizzle of extra-virgin olive oil. (The olive oil is essential to the flavor of the recipe—do not skip.) You can also garnish with Parmesan.

Strings Roasted Red Pepper Bisque

Noel Cunningham, chef/owner of Strings, is one of the nicest and most philanthropic restaurateurs around. This easy, delicious soup is one of the signature dishes at the ever-popular restaurant.

SERVES 6 TO 8

Wash and dry peppers. Cut into quarters (approximately), core, and seed. Place pieces flesh side down on baking sheet and brush them with olive oil. Reserve remaining oil.

Sprinkle pieces with kosher salt and coarsely ground pepper and place directly under broiler for about 5 minutes or until nicely charred. Place peppers in a closed plastic bag and let them sweat. Allow to cool; peel off the skins, then cut pieces into chunks.

In a large, heavy soup pot (about 5 quarts), heat remaining olive oil over medium heat; add more if needed to cover bottom of pot. Add roasted peppers and tomatoes. Cook until the juices release and aroma rises, then add the carrots, onion, and garlic. Sweat the vegetables over low heat just until onions and garlic are translucent but not browned.

4 red bell peppers
1/4 cup olive oil
1 teaspoon each kosher salt and
    coarsely ground pepper
6 ripe Roma tomatoes, cored and quartered
3 carrots, roughly cut
1 onion, roughly cut
2 large cloves garlic, peeled and sliced
1 quart chicken stock
1 cup heavy cream or half-and-half
Salt and white pepper to taste

Pour chicken stock over vegetables and bring to a boil. Reduce heat, cover, and gently simmer for 30 minutes. When done, turn off heat and, using a hand blender, puree the soup. In another pot, over medium heat reduce the cream or half-and-half by about half. Strain the pureed soup into the cream and season to taste with salt and white pepper.

Cook's Tip: *You can serve the bisque in large soup bowls as a main dish with garlic bread and salad as accompaniments. As a main dish, the recipe makes 4 to 6 servings.*

· ·

Racines Roasted Red Pepper Bisque

The folks at Racines like to rotate their soups daily. The Roasted Red Pepper Bisque is part of that rotation.

SERVES 6

Choose red bell peppers with smooth surfaces for easier peeling once roasted. Lightly rub with olive oil and season with salt and pepper. Grill over open flame or under broiler, turning peppers every 3 to 5 minutes until skins are blackened all over.

Place roasted peppers in large bowl and cover tightly with plastic wrap. Let cool for 1 hour. When cool, remove core, seeds, and skins. Peel under cool running water to remove skin more easily.

Refrigerate finished peppers until ready to add them to the bisque.

In soup pot, sauté onion, carrot, celery, and potatoes in a little olive oil over medium-high heat until slightly browned. Deglaze pot with the wine. Add cream, milk, water, tomato paste, bay leaf, and seasoning. Gently simmer on low heat until potatoes are done.

5 red bell peppers
Olive oil for roasting and sautéing
1 small yellow onion, diced
1 large carrot, sliced
1 stalk celery, sliced
2 potatoes, diced
1/4 cup white wine
1 pint heavy cream
1 cup milk
1 cup water
5 tablespoons tomato paste
1 bay leaf
Salt and white pepper to taste

Remove bay leaf and add peppers. Puree mixture in successive portions in blender and pour back into the soup pot. Reheat and adjust seasoning to taste.

Note: Recipe can be doubled.

· ·

Creamy Minestrone Soup

Jack Leone was the owner of Café Giovanni, Al Fresco, and Cucina Leone. Now he lives in Detroit, where he has opened Cucina Leone.

1 pound dried Great Northern white beans
5 14$^{1}/_{2}$-ounce cans beef broth
1 12-ounce piece salt pork
1 stick butter ($^{1}/_{4}$ pound or $^{1}/_{2}$ cup)
1 14$^{1}/_{2}$-ounce can crushed tomatoes
1 large yellow onion, diced
3 carrots, diced
$^{1}/_{2}$ cup sliced celery
1 tablespoon minced garlic
2 tablespoons olive oil
$^{1}/_{4}$ pound prosciutto, chopped
1 zucchini, sliced
1 yellow squash, sliced
4 Roma tomatoes, diced
$^{1}/_{2}$ cup cabbage, cut in thin strips
$^{1}/_{2}$ cup small dried pasta shells
$^{1}/_{4}$ cup fresh basil
2 tablespoons Italian seasoning
$^{1}/_{2}$ teaspoon pepper
1$^{1}/_{2}$ teaspoons red pepper flakes
1 pint heavy cream

SERVES 8 TO 10

Sort through the dried beans to remove any stones. Soak the beans overnight, according to package directions. Drain the beans and place in a large soup pot. Add broth, the whole piece of salt pork, and butter and simmer beans, covered, on low heat for 1 hour. Add 1 cup of hot water and simmer for another half-hour.

Remove the salt pork; add the crushed tomatoes, onion, carrots, celery, garlic, olive oil, and prosciutto. Cover again and simmer on low for 30 minutes. Add all remaining ingredients except cream and simmer for an additional 15 minutes.

Remove from heat, add the heavy cream, and then cool the soup. Store refrigerated overnight to allow the flavors to meld. Reheat and serve.

Cook's Tip: Leone uses ham stock instead of beef broth (you can create your own ham stock with bouillon cubes), but it's fine to use the more convenient substitute. Because salt pork varies in saltiness, you may want to use unsalted beef broth.

Steak Soup

The popular Trinity Grille uses cubes of tenderloin for this recipe. This is a filling soup, along the lines of a hearty vegetable beef soup.

SERVES 6 TO 8

Sear beef cubes on all sides until browned. Remove cubes and set aside. In same pan, melt butter and sauté carrots, onion, and celery until almost tender.

Add $1/4$ cup beef stock, herbs and spices, and flour and whisk vigorously to avoid lumps. Add the remaining beef broth and whisk.

Mix in beef, tomatoes, potatoes, peas, and Tabasco sauce. Simmer 20 minutes. Adjust salt and pepper. Serve.

1 pound sirloin steak, cubed
$1/2$ stick butter (2 ounces or $1/4$ cup)
2 carrots, diced large
1 large onion, diced large
2 stalks celery, diced large
5 cups rich beef broth,
    plus an additional $1/4$ cup
$1/2$ teaspoon oregano
$1/2$ teaspoon thyme
$1/4$ teaspoon granulated garlic
$1/2$ tablespoon pepper
$1/4$ cup flour
$1/4$ cup canned crushed tomatoes
$1/4$ cup canned diced tomatoes
$1/2$ pound potatoes, diced and cooked
$1/2$ cup fresh or frozen peas
$1/2$ teaspoon Tabasco sauce
Salt and pepper to taste

Larry's Cuban Black Bean Soup

This soup looks like a lot of work at first glance, but once you assemble and chop all the ingredients, you should be good to go.

SERVES 8 TO 10

Soak beans overnight in enough cold water to cover. Drain and set aside. Or do a quick soak: Bring 2 quarts of water to a boil. Add beans and continue to boil for a few minutes. Cover, remove from heat, and soak for 1 hour. Drain and set aside.

Finely chop tasso and andouille. Dice bacon and keep separate.

In a 5-quart soup pot, brown the bacon over medium heat until almost crisp; add the garlic and sauté, covered, but do not brown. Deglaze the pot (scraping up any browned bits) with sherry and reduce the liquid by half. Add the stock, water, beans, and remaining ingredients except cilantro and sour cream to the pot. Simmer until beans are tender, about $1^1/2$ to 2 hours.

1 pound dried black beans
2 quarts water
4 ounces tasso
4 ounces andouille
4 strips bacon
2 tablespoons finely minced fresh garlic
$1/4$ cup dry sherry
$3^1/2$ cups homemade chicken stock or canned broth
$3^1/2$ cups water
$1/2$ cup diced red onion
$1/2$ cup diced green bell pepper
$1/2$ cup diced celery
$1/2$ cup diced carrot
$1^1/2$ tablespoons ground cumin
$1/2$ tablespoon chopped fresh oregano
$1^1/2$ tablespoons chopped fresh basil
2 tablespoons chopped fresh cilantro
1 tablespoon ground pepper
3 tablespoons finely chopped fresh cilantro
1 cup sour cream

(continued on next page)

(Note: For creamier soup, puree half of soup mixture in blender for 15 seconds and return it to the pot.) Add 2 tablespoons of the cilantro.

Ladle soup into individual bowls and top each serving with a dollop of sour cream and a pinch of the remaining cilantro.

Cook's Tip: This recipe calls for tasso, which is a smoked, dried, and spiced pork used for seasoning in Cajun cooking. You may have to order it from a butcher, although it's often found at specialty grocery stores. Andouille is a highly spiced smoked pork sausage, also a common ingredient in Cajun dishes.

Polenta Soup

This is a very unusual soup that will keep your guests guessing about ingredients. Mascarpone, an Italian cream cheese most famous for its use in tiramisù, is sold in a round container at the specialty cheese counter of the grocery store.

SERVES 6

Combine liquids in a heavy nonstick pan with 1 tablespoon of salt and bring to a boil. Slowly whisk the cornmeal into the liquid, stirring constantly. Continue stirring for 5 minutes over high heat, then reduce to a simmer. (Be careful; if the heat is too high, the mixture will splatter.) Continue to cook the mixture for 20 minutes, stirring frequently; then fold in the mascarpone and the butter. Season to taste.

Garnish the top of the soup with shaved Parmesan, radicchio, parsley sprigs.

3 cups skim milk
3 cups water or chicken stock (preferable)
1 tablespoon salt
1 cup cornmeal
1/2 cup mascarpone
2 tablespoons butter
Salt and freshly ground pepper to taste
2 ounces shaved Parmesan for garnish
1 small head radicchio, julienned, for garnish
Italian parsley sprigs for garnish

Onion Soup

When I looked at the ingredients for this recipe and saw oxtails, I thought, "Oh boy!" Then I walked right into the grocery store and there they were in the meat counter. Oxtails (which don't really come from oxen, but from beef cattle) are prized for their rich, beefy flavor and for their thick consistency when cooked. They need to be braised, which will tenderize them. Just to be on the safe side, I'd order the oxtails from the grocery or butcher, just so you know that you'll find them. This is an absolutely delicious version of the classic.

SERVES 8 TO 10

Place oxtails with water into a covered pot such as a dutch oven and braise in oven at 400 degrees for about 1 hour or until well-browned.

Add beef stock, reduce heat to 250 degrees, and cook, covered, for about 1 hour. Meanwhile, sauté onions in butter until well browned and caramelized, stirring frequently, 20 to 30 minutes. Off the heat, add the brandy. Return the pan to the heat and light with a long fireplace match, being careful because mixture is volatile and will flame up quickly. Carefully flame onions in brandy until flame is out. (The fire cooks out the alcohol content of the brandy, but leaves its rich flavor behind.)

2 pounds oxtails
1 cup water
2 quarts rich beef stock
2 onions, diced
1 stick butter ($1/4$ pound or $1/2$ cup)
$1/4$ cup brandy
Toasted croutons or french bread slices
Grated provolone

Strain oxtail mixture, discarding bones, into onions and simmer on low heat for 10 minutes. Pour into individual ovenproof soup bowls and top each bowl of soup with toasted croutons or toasted french bread slices. (You can place an empty bowl over each bread slice and trim to fit.) Place provolone on top of bread and run soup under hot broiler for a moment until cheese is melted and golden.

Cook's Tip: Braising is a slow-cooking technique, which, when applied to a tough cut of meat, will tenderize such cuts, as well as concentrate flavor. The meat is placed in a small amount of water, with a lid on the pot—which bastes the meat. Because of that, this soup takes a couple hours to prepare.

Spinach Soup

Markus P. Georg, at the lovely family-owned Chinook Tavern, has made this recipe as home cook–friendly as possible. The soup's creamy texture is created by the addition of a roux—a mixture of flour and butter.

SERVES 4

Heat the butter in a pot over moderate heat. Add the flour all at once. Whisking constantly, cook over low heat until the roux is blond, approximately 8 minutes.

Bring the chicken stock to a boil. Whip the roux into the stock to eliminate any lumps. Simmer for 30 minutes, whisking frequently.

Add spinach and bring the soup back to a simmer. Remove from stove and puree. Put the soup back on the stove; bring to a simmer; and season to taste with salt, white pepper, and nutmeg.

Garnish with unsweetened whipped cream and croutons.

1 stick butter ($1/4$ pound or $1/2$ cup)
1 cup all-purpose flour
2 quarts chicken stock
10 ounces fresh spinach, washed and patted dry
Salt, white pepper, and nutmeg to taste
Unsweetened whipped cream for garnish (optional)
Croutons for garnish

Cook's Tip: The roux, which can range from white to brown, depending on how long you cook it, is the key to many dishes. Used for thickening, the roux is also cooked for a shorter or longer time to impart flavor and color to the dish. In this case, you want to allow it to cook until pale in color and the mixture doesn't have a floury taste. The secret to roux is to let it cook slowly. Watch it carefully on the stove, but don't rush it along.

Green Chili

Green chili is probably our number-one request, but many restaurants consider it a signature dish and don't want to divulge their secrets. Chopper's makes this version of a medium-hot green chili with the secret ingredient of granulated garlic as its special touch. (You'll find granulated garlic in the spice section of the grocery store.)

SERVES 6

In a covered medium pot, simmer pork in salted water until tender, about $1^1/2$ hours.

In a large, heavy pot over medium heat, melt butter. Add onion, oregano, and granulated garlic. Sweat the onion until softened. (To sweat the onion, merely cover it and cook over low heat.)

Stir flour into the onion mixture to make a roux, stirring constantly, and adding a little more butter if needed. Cook roux until lightly browned. Add chicken broth, a little at a time,

2 pounds diced pork
1 teaspoon salt
$5^1/2$ cups water
1 stick butter ($^1/4$ pound or $^1/2$ cup)
$^1/2$ large yellow onion, diced
$^1/2$ teaspoon oregano
$1^1/2$ teaspoons granulated garlic
$^3/4$ cup flour
$2^1/2$ cups chicken broth
1 7-ounce can Hatch hot chiles, drained and chopped
2 7-ounce cans Hatch mild chiles, drained and chopped
1 tablespoon chili powder

whisking until smooth. Add the chiles, chili powder, and the pork—including all the cooking liquid.

Gently simmer mixture, stirring occasionally, until thickened. Serve.

Pearl Street Grill

Chicken Tortilla Soup

This restaurant, with its menu featuring every-thing from fish and chips to sandwiches to Mexican-style food, is a crowd-pleasing favorite.

SERVES 8

Bring the chicken stock and tomato juice to a boil, lower heat to simmer, add tomato, carrot, garlic, onion, chiles, and cumin. (If you want vegetables slightly crunchy, put directly into simmering soup for 30 minutes. If you want them softer, sauté them first in a couple table-spoons of oil and then add to the soup.) Add the cooked chicken to the soup to heat. Add the cilantro and basil. Ladle soup into individual bowls and top with tortilla chips, cheese, avo-cado, and tomato.

Cook's Tip: *Use serranos if you want a hotter soup.*

2 quarts chicken stock
23 ounces tomato juice
1 cup diced tomato
1 carrot, julienned
1 1/2 tablespoons chopped garlic
1/2 red onion, julienned
5 serranos or jalapeños, diced and seeded, or combination
Pinch cumin
2 boneless, skinless chicken breasts, poached and sliced very thin
1/2 cup chopped fresh cilantro
1/4 cup chopped fresh basil
Monterey Jack cheese for garnish
Tortilla chips for garnish
Avocado slices for garnish
Diced fresh tomato for garnish

Southwestern Corn Chowder

Karen Mulholland of the charming Karen's in the Country is a wonderful cook, and this soup is really good. This is one of several requests that we received for recipes from her restaurant.

SERVES 6

Melt butter with onion in a 2½-quart pot and cook over low heat until translucent (5 to 7 minutes). Add flour and cook until mixture turns a light golden color—a blond roux.

Add chicken stock, bouquet garni, heavy cream, and potato; bring to a slow simmer. Let simmer for 20 to 25 minutes, stirring occasionally. Add corn and green chiles and simmer 10 more minutes.

Remove bouquet garni and pour soup into bowls. Garnish each bowl of soup with a tablespoon of Pico de Gallo.

1 stick butter (¼ pound or ½ cup)
½ yellow onion, diced
½ cup flour
1 quart chicken stock
1 bouquet garni (2 bay leaves, 10 whole peppercorns, 2 cloves garlic, thyme sprig, and parsley stem wrapped in coffee filter and tied with string)
2 cups heavy cream
1 medium red potato, diced (skin on)
2 cups canned corn (not creamed), drained
1 cup diced green chiles
Pico de Gallo for garnish (see recipe that follows)

Pico de Gallo

MAKES ½ CUP

Mix all ingredients and set aside.

1 tomato, finely diced
½ yellow onion, finely diced
½ jalapeño, seeded, finely diced
10 to 12 sprigs of cilantro, chopped

Clam Chowder

Most clam chowder recipes call for some kind of bacon or salt pork. This one takes its flavors from the combination of milk, half-and-half, clams, and vegetables. Season generously with hot pepper sauce.

SERVES 8

Sauté onion in butter. When onions are transparent but not brown, add celery, bell peppers, and the garlic and sauté.

When vegetables are soft but not browned, add corn and chopped clams and their juice. Cook for 10 minutes. Add sherry; bring to a boil and cook for 10 minutes, stirring occasionally, until reduced. Lower temperature. Add milk and half-and-half and potatoes. Allow to simmer; do not boil.

In a skillet, melt butter and whisk in flour to make a roux. Cook on low to medium heat, stirring until it becomes a deep blond color; do not allow mixture to become too brown.

Add the roux to the clam mixture. When it starts to thicken, remove from heat and add spices. Simmer 10 minutes, stirring constantly— do not boil. Add hot pepper sauce to taste. Ladle into individual bowls and sprinkle with fresh basil.

$1^{1}/_{2}$ medium yellow onions, chopped
2 tablespoons butter
3 stalks celery, chopped
1 green bell pepper, chopped
1 red bell pepper, chopped
1 tablespoon chopped garlic
$^{1}/_{4}$ cup frozen corn, thawed
4 cups chopped clams and their juice
   (4 10-ounce cans)
$^{1}/_{4}$ cup sherry
2 cups 2 percent milk
2 cups half-and-half
6 red potatoes, skin on, cut into small cubes
$^{1}/_{4}$ cup flour
$^{1}/_{4}$ cup butter
$^{1}/_{2}$ tablespoon pepper
$^{1}/_{8}$ teaspoon nutmeg
$^{1}/_{8}$ teaspoon paprika
Hot pepper sauce, such as Tabasco, to taste
3 tablespoons julienned fresh basil
   for garnish

Fisherman's Stew

Luigi's uses salmon, shrimp, mussels, and calamari, but any combination of seafood is acceptable. This is an absolutely delicious recipe. I used sea bass, shrimp, and mussels. A traditional brodetto or fisherman's stew is served over bread. I would put a slice of toasted or grilled Italian bread on the bottom of the bowl. Short of that, serve a good, crusty bread alongside.

SERVES 8

Simmer sun-dried tomatoes in the water for 15 to 20 minutes or until soft. Do not discard water. Remove sun-dried tomatoes from water with a slotted spoon, chop, and set aside.

Sauté onions, peppers, and garlic in olive oil until soft. Do not brown.

Add remaining ingredients (including water retained from sun-dried tomatoes), except for fresh parsley, basil, and seafood, and simmer for 30 minutes.

Add desired seafood such as mussels, clams, shrimp, salmon, whitefish, crab, calamari, or scallops, and fresh herbs. (Keep in mind that

$1/2$ cup sun-dried tomatoes
$1^1/2$ cups water
1 small white onion, diced
$1/3$ of a green bell pepper, diced
$1/3$ of a red bell pepper, diced
3 cloves garlic, minced
1 tablespoon olive oil
1 15-ounce can tomato sauce
1 28-ounce can crushed Roma tomatoes
1 cup white wine, such as sauvignon blanc
$2^2/3$ cups chicken stock, preferably unsalted
1 teaspoon oregano
$3/4$ teaspoon marjoram
$3/4$ teaspoon crushed red pepper flakes
$1/4$ teaspoon thyme
1 tablespoon kosher salt
$1/2$ teaspoon pepper
$1/2$ cup chopped fresh parsley (optional)
1 tablespoon julienned fresh basil
2 pounds of assorted seafood, such as
    $1/2$ pound peeled, deveined shrimp;
    $1/2$ pound sea bass, diced; $1/2$ pound
    scallops; $1/2$ pound mussels
    (or any seafood of your choice)

for certain shellfish—such as mussels, shrimp, calamari, and scallops—a briefer cooking time of 2 to 3 minutes is preferred to ensure tenderness.) Simmer seafood in broth, covered, about 10 minutes.

Serve immediately with a good sourdough bread or polenta, or over bread or pasta.

Note: If using mussels, clean and "de-beard" if necessary by yanking out the tough black threads. Discard any mussels that are broken. Also, discard any mussels that do not open during cooking.

Cook's Tip: You can also borrow a page from the Cioppino recipe that follows and serve it over capellini or linguine.

Cioppino

Dale Filson Jr., executive chef of Pesce Fresco, gave us this delicious recipe. The chef recommends a brand of sherry such as that produced by Paul Masson Winery. I happened to have Harveys Bristol Cream on hand, so I used that. The broth was slightly sweet and flavorful. The chef also ladles the cioppino on top of cooked capellini. You can use any kind of seafood that strikes your fancy.

SERVES 2 TO 4,
DEPENDING ON SERVING SIZE

Sauté scallops and diced fish in 2 tablespoons butter for 2 to 3 minutes. Remove seafood.

Deglaze the pan with sherry, scraping up any browned bits, and bring to a boil.

Add clam juice and tomato sauce; season. Add scallops and fish, mussels and shrimp, cover and continue to simmer just until fish is cooked and mussels have opened. (Discard any that do not open.)

Adjust seasonings. Pour over capellini pasta in shallow bowls. Serve with focaccia.

4 large scallops
1/2 pound diced fish
    (suggested types to combine:
    salmon, swordfish, mahimahi, sea bass)
2 tablespoons butter
3/4 cup dry sherry
1/2 cup plus 1 tablespoon of
    good quality clam juice or fish stock
3/4 cup tomato sauce
Salt and pepper to taste
Crushed red pepper to taste
8 mussels
12 shrimp
Cooked capellini pasta, enough for 4
Grilled focaccia bread as accompaniment

Gumbo

Wynkoop is known for its beers, its bangers and mash, its shepherd pie, and its owner, Mayor John Hickenlooper. Gumbo is the kind of hearty one-dish meal that lends itself very nicely to a complementary microbrew.

SERVES 6 TO 8

1 pound boneless, skinless
   chicken breasts or thighs
$1/2$ pound cod or catfish
$3/4$ pound andouille
$1/4$ cup canola oil
$1^1/2$ cups chopped yellow onion
   (about 1 medium-sized)
$1^1/2$ cups chopped green bell pepper (about
   1 large)
2 tablespoons minced garlic
   (about 3 to 4 cloves)
$1/4$ cup flour

2 8-ounce bottles of clam juice,
   plus $1/4$ cup tomato juice or water
4 cups tomato juice
$3^1/2$ teaspoons Tabasco
1 teaspoon cayenne
$1/2$ pound shrimp
1 teaspoon salt
1 teaspoon pepper
1 tablespoon filé powder
Cooked rice for 6 to 8
   (approximately 1 cup per serving)
2 bunches green onions, chopped, for
   garnish

Cut chicken and fish into bite-sized cubes; keep separate and set aside. Slice sausage and set aside. Heat oil in large saucepan until very hot, but not smoking.

Carefully add chicken and brown on all sides. Stir in peppers and onions until they begin to wilt (about 5 minutes). Add flour and mix well, cook another five minutes. Add clam

(continued on next page)

juice, tomato juice, Tabasco, cayenne, and sausage, bring to a boil, then lower heat to a simmer and cook for about 30 minutes. (If gumbo seems dry, add some water.)

Add shrimp and fish and cook for a few minutes until just done (about 5 minutes). Add salt, pepper, and filé powder. Taste and adjust seasonings if necessary. Serve gumbo over cooked rice in bowls. Sprinkle on chopped green onions and additional filé powder if desired.

Cook's Tip: *Filé powder is an ingredient essential to creole gumbo, with a distinctive main ingredient—sassafras—plus dried okra, allspice, coriander, and sage.*

Salads

Crab Salad with Lemon Basil Vinaigrette   57

Jumbo Prawn and Portobello Mushroom Salad   59

Spinach Salad with Sweet-and-Sour Honey Ginger Dressing   60

Spinach Salad with Orange Hazelnut Vinaigrette   61

Spinach Salad with Pear and Gorgonzola   63

Basil and Pine Nut Pasta Salad   64

Mixed Greens with Penne and Grilled Chicken and Lemon Basil Vinaigrette   65

Cajun Chicken Salad   67

Steak Salad   68

Organic Greens with Herbed Chevre and Sun-Dried Cherry Vinaigrette   69

Red Ranch Dressing   71

Roasted Garlic Ranch Dressing   72

Caesar Salad Dressing   73

Grilled Tomato Vinaigrette   74

Crab Salad with Lemon Basil Vinaigrette

Avenue Grill has some wonderful salads on the menu. This one takes crab salad to a more interesting dimension, by adding a bed of salad greens tossed with a Lemon Basil Vinaigrette.

SERVES 4 TO 6

Combine first 6 ingredients in bowl. Adjust seasonings to taste.

Spoon vinaigrette over greens, tomatoes, cucumbers, and olives and mix lightly. Spoon crab salad mixture over salad greens; top with thinly sliced red onions and roasted red peppers, if desired.

Cook's Tip: It can be a treat to use fresh Dungeness crab for this recipe, which has a very sweet and juicy flesh. Dungeness is in season in the winter/spring months. If you buy the crabs whole in the seafood section of such groceries as Whole Foods, you can ask the seafood personnel to clean and crack the crab (buying them this way can cut the cost of this delicacy at least in half).

1 pound fresh or canned snow crab meat
3 ribs of celery, finely diced
3 tablespoons finely chopped red onion
$1/3$ cup mayonnaise
Scant $1/2$ teaspoon Old Bay Seasoning, or to taste
$1/4$ teaspoon pepper
Lemon Basil Vinaigrette (see recipe that follows)
Organic spring greens
4 or 5 Roma tomatoes, chopped or cut in wedges
2 cucumbers, sliced
8 black olives, pitted (kalamata olives are recommended)
Red onions, thinly sliced (optional)
Roasted red peppers (optional)

(continued on next page)

Lemon Basil Vinaigrette

<small>MAKES 2 CUPS</small>

Put everything but oils and Parmesan in a blender or food processor and whirl 30 seconds. Add the oils in a slow, steady stream. When mixture is blended, add Parmesan and blend another 30 seconds.

$^1/_4$ cup fresh lemon juice
$^1/_4$ cup white balsamic vinegar or white wine vinegar
2 shallots
1 garlic clove
3 tablespoons honey
$^1/_4$ cup fresh basil leaves
2 tablespoons Dijon mustard
$^1/_2$ teaspoon salt
$^1/_4$ teaspoon red chili flakes
1 cup olive oil
$^1/_2$ cup vegetable oil
$^1/_4$ cup Parmesan

Jumbo Prawn and Portobello Mushroom Salad

We have no end of requests for recipes from Executive Chef Stephen Vice of McCormick's. The jumbo prawns, although expensive, are usually split along the shell, making them easy to peel. This is a beautiful, colorful, and delicious salad.

SERVES 4

Preheat oven to 375 degrees.

To prepare mushrooms, clean out the gills by scraping with a tablespoon. Briefly marinate cleaned caps in a mixture of 3 tablespoons balsamic vinegar, 2 tablespoons olive oil, and salt and pepper to taste.

Place mushrooms on a cookie sheet with sides or similar shallow pan and roast in oven for 15 minutes or until golden brown and tender. Remove from oven, cool, and slice each cap into fourths.

To prepare prawns, preheat broiler or prepare outdoor grill. Brush cleaned prawns with lemon butter (4 tablespoons melted butter and the juice of half a large lemon or a whole small one) and season with salt and pepper. Place under broiler or on the grill for 2 to 4 minutes per side, basting every 1 to 2 minutes with the lemon butter, until cooked through.

4 portobello mushrooms, stems removed
2 tablespoons olive oil
3 tablespoons balsamic vinegar
Salt and pepper to taste
12 to 16 jumbo prawns, peeled, deveined, and tails removed
4 tablespoons butter, melted
2 lemons
  (cut one of the lemons into 4 wedges)
10 ounces fresh baby spinach, washed and patted dry
1 cup good-quality balsamic vinaigrette or make your own: use $3/4$ cup olive oil to $1/4$ cup balsamic vinegar
2 ripe tomatoes, cut into 8 wedges
$1/2$ cup crumbled goat cheese
2 tablespoons chopped fresh parsley (optional)

Place spinach in a large bowl and toss with vinaigrette; divide evenly among four individual salad plates. Arrange prawns, tomato wedges, and portobello mushroom slices on top of spinach. Finish each salad with an ounce of crumbled goat cheese and a sprinkling of chopped parsley. Garnish each plate with a wedge of lemon.

Spinach Salad with Sweet-and-Sour Honey Ginger Dressing

Ed Novak is one of the best-known restaurateurs in Denver. His restaurants are known for the famous shrimp bowl that starts every meal, although this recipe is not far behind it in popularity.

SERVES 8

Toss spinach and dressing together, then divide equally among 8 serving plates and top each salad with remaining ingredients.

Cook's Tip: Note that the dressing will serve 8 (or more), but the ingredients for the salad are given in individual proportions because once you toss the spinach and dressing, the other ingredients are "composed" on top. Any leftover dressing can be refrigerated for 2 to 3 days and reused.

Sweet-and-Sour Honey Ginger Dressing

MAKES 2 CUPS

Mix all ingredients and simmer on the stove for 5 minutes, or until sugar is completely dissolved. Cool 15 minutes.

6 ounces fresh spinach or baby spinach (about $3/4$ ounce per person), washed, patted dry, and stemmed
2 ounces per serving of Sweet-and-Sour Honey Ginger Dressing (see recipe that follows)
2 cups mandarin orange segments
1 cup thinly sliced red onions
1 cup sliced mushrooms
1 cup coarsely chopped walnuts

$1^1/2$ teaspoons dry mustard
1 cup white vinegar
4 tablespoons soy sauce
1 tablespoon minced garlic
4 teaspoons grated gingerroot
$1/2$ cup olive oil
3 tablespoons sesame oil
$1/8$ cup fresh lemon juice
3 tablespoons sugar
3 tablespoons honey
2 teaspoons salt
2 teaspoons pepper

Spinach Salad with Orange Hazelnut Vinaigrette

Chef Jennifer Jasinski, who has always been great about sharing recipes, was happy to add this spinach salad. Note that the dressing takes an hour to reduce and the hazelnuts take about 45 minutes, so plan ahead.

SERVES 8

Toss the baby spinach, shaved fennel, and red onion together in a mixing bowl with the vinaigrette. Divide salad evenly among 8 plates and arrange the citrus segments around the salad so that their colors alternate. Top with the candied hazelnuts.

12 ounces baby spinach, washed and
   patted dry
2 cups shaved fennel
1 cup shaved red onion
Orange Hazelnut Vinaigrette
   (see recipe that follows)
3 whole oranges, divided into segments
   (about 3 segments per serving)
3 whole ruby red grapefruits, divided into
   segments (about 3 segments per serving)
Candied Hazelnuts
   (see recipe that follows)

Orange Hazelnut Vinaigrette

MAKES 2 CUPS

In a small saucepan over medium heat, cook the quart of orange juice and the sugar until reduced to about $^3/_4$ cup—it will take about an hour. Set aside and cool.

In a blender, add the reduced orange juice mixture, egg yolk, and sherry vinegar. Turn the blender on and slowly pour the oils into the blender to emulsify. As the mixture thickens,

1 quart orange juice
$^1/_2$ cup sugar
1 egg yolk
2 tablespoons sherry vinegar
1 cup peanut oil
$^1/_2$ cup, plus 2 tablespoons hazelnut oil
$^1/_2$ cup fresh orange juice
Salt and black pepper to taste
$1^1/_2$ tablespoons chopped shallots

(continued on next page)

thin out by adding the fresh orange juice. After all the oil has been incorporated, season to taste with salt and pepper. Pour the vinaigrette into a container and stir in the chopped shallots.

Candied Hazelnuts

MAKES 1½ CUPS

Combine all ingredients except oil in a 3-quart pot and stir to dissolve sugar. Cook on low heat at a slow boil until the sugar syrup becomes thick around the nuts. (It takes about 45 minutes.) Immediately remove pan from heat. Fry in hot peanut oil (using a candy thermometer, heat should not exceed 320 degrees) in a deep wok, fryer, or heavy high-sided pan until the

Note: If you are concerned about the use of raw egg, substitute one of the pasteurized egg products.

1 cup water
1 cup sugar
1½ cups hazelnuts
2 cups peanut oil for frying

nuts are golden brown. Remove nuts from oil with slotted spoon or similar tool and let them cool; be sure to keep the nuts separated from each other or they will stick together.

Spinach Salad with Pear and Gorgonzola

Even though the salad isn't on the menu anymore, Restaurateur Randy Rutherford of the Larimer Group, which owns Josephina's, secured the recipe for us. This is a hearty salad that you could eat as a main dish.

SERVES 2

Poach and grill pear halves. Whisk together balsamic vinegar, olive oil, and kosher salt to form a simple vinaigrette. Toss spinach and greens in dressing and set aside. Divide greens equally between 2 plates, then place pear halves on top of greens. Pear should be served warm. Top greens with Gorgonzola and walnuts.

Arrange fennel and tomatoes decoratively around salad.

Note: Poach pear in 1 cup water, 1/2 cup white wine, and a cinnamon stick for 10 minutes; cool in poaching liquid. Remove pear, then broil or grill for a few minutes to finish. (The grilling caramelizes the natural sugars in the pear.)

1 pear, peeled, cored, and halved
2 tablespoons balsamic vinegar
4 tablespoons olive oil
Pinch of kosher salt
1 cup baby spinach, washed and patted dry
1 cup field greens, washed and patted dry
1/4 cup crumbled Gorgonzola
2 tablespoons chopped toasted walnuts
1/4 cup fennel, julienned and blanched
    (place in boiling water for a moment,
    then place in a bowl of cold water)
2 Roma tomatoes, chopped

Cook's Tip: Fennel has an anise or licorice-flavored taste. It looks like celery stuck in an onion, with feathery leaves on top. Pull off the tough outer layer of the bulb and cut the bulb into matchstick-size pieces for this recipe.

Basil and Pine Nut Pasta Salad

Easy? Yes. This simple, tasty pasta dish would make a nice addition to a buffet or even a picnic. You can buy fresh pasta at Pasta, Pasta, Pasta or you can substitute with the grocery store brands. Or, of course, you could make your own.

SERVES 6

Cook the fresh pasta 3 minutes in boiling salted water, or cook according to package directions. Drain. Place pasta in a bowl, add a little olive oil, and toss several times while it cools, so that the pasta strands won't stick together.

When cooled, add salt and pepper to taste and Parmesan. Add an additional 2 to 3 tablespoons olive oil and the pine nuts and salt and pepper to taste. Turn onto a platter and sprinkle with chopped fresh basil.

Serve immediately.

1 pound fresh thin spaghetti
   (or 1 package of a fresh grocery store
   brand, angel hair pasta or similar)
3 to 4 tablespoons olive oil
Salt and pepper to taste
1/2 cup grated Parmesan
1/4 to 1/2 cup pine nuts, toasted, if desired
Chopped fresh basil for garnish

Cook's Tip: Although Pasta, Pasta, Pasta does not toast the pine nuts, if you prefer them toasted, place on a baking sheet and toast for a few minutes at 300 degrees. Watch carefully so nuts don't burn.

Mixed Greens with Penne and Grilled Chicken and Lemon Basil Vinaigrette

Augustine Grill is located in a cool house that originally was built as a private home in 1907. The Linneys have owned it for the past 8 years and the food is top-notch. In this recipe, which is perfect for summer, field greens, pasta, and chicken are combined in one dish.

SERVES 8

Marinate chicken breasts in marinade in refrigerator, covered, for at least 2 hours, or overnight. Remove chicken from marinade and discard marinade. Grill chicken.

In a stainless-steel bowl, toss the greens with diced tomato and shredded jicama. Arrange the greens on each plate, top with pasta, and generously drizzle on the Lemon Basil Vinaigrette. Top with grilled chicken and serve.

Marinade

$^1/_4$ cup tarragon vinegar
$^1/_3$ cup olive oil
1 tablespoon tarragon
4 sprigs fresh tarragon, minced
1 teaspoon minced garlic
1 sprig rosemary, minced

8 boneless, skinless chicken breast halves
Marinade (see recipe that follows)
Field greens (enough to serve 8)
4 medium tomatoes, diced
1 jicama bulb, peeled and shredded
12 ounces dried penne pasta, cooked
Lemon Basil Vinaigrette
   (see recipe that follows)

Cook's Tip: Jicama looks like a big brown knotty ball. Because of its size, supermarkets often sell it cut in half. To use, peel off the brown skin. Its texture is crunchy like a water chestnut and it can be diced or julienned. It's an excellent addition to a fresh vegetable tray.

MAKES ABOUT $^1/_2$ CUP

Whisk together all ingredients.

(continued on next page)

Lemon Basil Vinaigrette

MAKES ABOUT 2^1/$_2$ CUPS

Put all ingredients in a food processor. Blend until smooth.

3 fresh basil leaves
2 to 3 garlic cloves
2 cups extra-virgin olive oil
^{1}/$_4$ cup pine nuts
^{1}/$_3$ cup fresh lemon juice
^{1}/$_8$ cup red wine vinegar
3 tablespoons pesto,
    commercial or homemade
^{1}/$_4$ teaspoon kosher salt
^{1}/$_2$ teaspoon ground pepper

. . . .

Cajun Chicken Salad

The Market is known for its delicious ready-to-go salads, soups, sandwiches, and bakery treats. Owner Mark Greenberg gave us this recipe and also one for the pumpkin chocolate chip cookies that have become a favorite around our house (see the Desserts chapter for this treat).

SERVES 8 TO 10

The day before: Place chicken breasts in a 9 × 13-inch glass baking dish. Whisk together olive oil, garlic, and ground pepper and brush both sides of chicken with the mixture. Sprinkle breasts with salt. Bake at 350 degrees until done, about 20 minutes on each side, turning halfway through. Cool, cover, and refrigerate.

Cut chicken into bite-sized pieces and put into a large bowl. Add remaining ingredients, except red pepper flakes, adding just enough mayonnaise to hold mixture together (mixture should not be soupy). Add red pepper flakes gradually, tasting to adjust for preferred seasoning. Salt and pepper to taste.

6 boneless, skinless chicken breast halves
1/3 cup olive oil
2 cloves garlic, minced
1/4 teaspoon coarsely ground pepper
Salt
1 medium red onion, finely diced
3 green onions, finely diced
1 large refrigerated dill pickle, diced
   (tested with Claussen whole
   kosher dills; use up to 3)
1 firm cucumber, peeled and diced
1 to 1 1/2 cups mayonnaise
   (more or less, to taste)
1/2 to 1 1/2 teaspoons red pepper chili flakes
Salt and pepper

Cook's Tip: As you add the red pepper chili flakes, go slowly, waiting for the kicky aftertaste before adding more.

Steak Salad

The dressing for this signature salad from Racines is bold and would be delicious on any kind of salad that features meats and cheeses.

SERVES 6

Prepare vinaigrette. Toss all ingredients except steak and dressing in large bowl. Arrange on individual plates.

Grill steak to desired degree of doneness. Slice steak against the grain of the meat in quarter-inch slices and arrange on top of salad. Drizzle desired amount of vinaigrette over salad and serve.

Balsamic Vinaigrette

MAKES ABOUT 4$^{1}/_{4}$ CUPS

Whisk or blend all ingredients, adding olive oil last in a steady stream, until mixture is emulsified.

15 ounces mixed field greens
3 fresh tomatoes, cut into wedges
2 carrots, sliced into coins (sliced rounds)
2 red bell peppers, julienned
4$^{1}/_{2}$ ounces blue cheese crumbles
15 black olives, pitted
    (kalamata or other, as preferred)
1 red onion, cut into rings
18 ounces sirloin steak
Balsamic Vinaigrette
    (see recipe that follows)

$^{1}/_{4}$ cup honey
1 cup Dijon mustard
1 cup balsamic vinegar
1 tablespoon fresh lemon juice
5 to 6 ounces water (adjust according
    to preference for thickness)
1 tablespoon chopped fresh rosemary
1 tablespoon chopped fresh basil
1 tablespoon chopped fresh thyme
2 tablespoons chopped fresh parsley
1 tablespoon minced garlic
Salt and pepper to taste
2 cups olive oil

Organic Greens with Herbed Chevre and Sun-Dried Cherry Vinaigrette

This salad combines some ingredients that have become popular in the past few years— chevre, or goat cheese, and sun-dried cherries. You can save a step these days by buying a pre-made herbed goat cheese log. Although sun-dried cherries are pricey, they're worth it. The salad and dressing wowed our guests at a dinner party.

SERVES 6

Prepare vinaigrette several hours in advance so that flavors will meld. When ready to assemble, roll a goat cheese log into chopped parsley, chives, and pepper (you can skip this step and substitute a prepared herbed goat cheese log). Wet a sharp knife under hot water and slice goat cheese in slices. Rinse knife between slices to keep cuts clean.

Slice baguette diagonally and brush slices with melted butter. Broil until golden; set aside.

Sun-dried Cherry Vinaigrette
  (see recipe that follows)
1 12-ounce package organic spring mix
   greens
5-ounce goat cheese log
1 tablespoon chopped fresh parsley
1 tablespoon chopped fresh chives
1 teaspoon pepper
1 baguette
Melted butter
Crumbled bacon for garnish
Chopped pecans for garnish
Chopped sun-dried cherries for garnish

Toss organic spring mix with vinaigrette and arrange in center of plate. Intersperse 3 slices of herbed goat cheese with 3 baguette slices around each serving of salad mixture.

Garnish with a sprinkling of bacon bits, pecans, and sun-dried cherries.

(continued on next page)

Sun-dried Cherry Vinaigrette

MAKES ABOUT 1^1/$_2$ CUPS

Simmer cherries, wine, vinegar, and 1 table-spoon of shallots in small saucepan until cherries are soft, about 2 minutes. Cool; then place in a blender and add all remaining ingredients except olive oil. Puree ingredients. Pour in olive oil gradually in a thin stream through the hole in the blender cap. Adjust salt and pepper to taste and chill.

^{1}/$_2$ cup sun-dried cherries
2 tablespoons chardonnay
^{1}/$_4$ cup red wine vinegar
3 tablespoons chopped shallots
3 tablespoons red wine vinegar
3 tablespoons honey
^{1}/$_4$ cup fresh basil leaves
^{1}/$_2$ teaspoon kosher salt
^{1}/$_4$ teaspoon ground pepper
1 cup olive oil

Red Ranch Dressing

This salad dressing is a staple of El Rancho, which is celebrating more than fifty years in business. Owners Bill Troyanos and Donna Piro, a husband-and-wife team, have a new signature item to add to the old favorites—elk and buffalo wontons.

MAKES ENOUGH DRESSING
FOR 12 SERVINGS

Combine diced and pureed onions with pureed beets and beet juice. Add lemon juice, salt, garlic, white pepper, basil, oregano, dehydrated onion, and sugar.

Whip mayonnaise, sour cream, and buttermilk by hand or with mixer. Add onion mixture and Hidden Valley Ranch mix to the mayonnaise, sour cream, and milk and stir until mixture is fully blended. Serve tossed with salad greens.

6 tablespoons pureed red onion
3 tablespoons finely diced red onion
2 tablespoons pureed beets
3 tablespoons beet juice
1 tablespoon fresh lemon juice
$1/2$ teaspoon salt
1 tablespoon garlic powder
$1/4$ teaspoon white pepper
$1/4$ teaspoon basil
$1/8$ teaspoon oregano
6 tablespoons dehydrated onion
Pinch of sugar
3 cups mayonnaise
1 cup sour cream
2 cups buttermilk
$1^1/2$ tablespoons Hidden Valley's Original
   Ranch Salad Dressing & Seasoning Mix
Salad greens of your choice

Roasted Garlic Ranch Dressing

Chef/owner Dave Query of Jax Fish House and Zolo Grill in Boulder has some of the most popular restaurants in the area. He's also the co-author (with Jill Zeh Richter) of *Jax Fish House Book of Fish*. At the restaurant, the dressing is served on a wedge of iceberg lettuce.

MAKES ENOUGH DRESSING
FOR 10 SERVINGS

Puree the garlic in the blender with a little of the buttermilk; then combine all remaining ingredients in a blender and blend until smooth.

Cook's Tip: To roast garlic, take 1 head of garlic, with the top third of it cut off and the loose papery peel removed. Place it on a sheet of heavy duty foil, sprinkle with olive oil, and seal the foil tightly. Roast in oven at 400 degrees for about 45 minutes. Remove from oven and cool. Roasted garlic has the consistency of butter and is easily squeezed from the skin of the cloves. You can mix leftover roasted garlic with butter and spread on French bread, or serve over hot cooked vegetables, such as broccoli.

1^1/$_2$ tablespoons pureed roasted garlic
1 cup buttermilk
1^1/$_2$ cups mayonnaise
^{1}/$_4$ cup chopped scallions
1 tablespoon chopped parsley
Pinch cayenne pepper
^{1}/$_2$ teaspoon black pepper
1 teaspoon kosher salt

Caesar Salad Dressing

Owner Mark Johnson of Luigi's Bent Noodle was kind enough to provide this recipe, which he cut down from a mega-batch. The recipe can be cut in half—or you can simply plan to refrigerate the leftovers for up to 2 days. Adjust the seasonings to taste.

MAKES ENOUGH DRESSING FOR
10 TO 12 SERVINGS

Puree onion, garlic cloves (if you like it really garlicky, use the whole amount), anchovies, mustard, lemon juice, Worcestershire sauce, and hot pepper sauce to a smooth paste in food processor.

Whip egg yolks and vinegar together in a blender. With blender running, slowly add oil through hole in lid until incorporated. Slowly incorporate garlic-anchovy mixture. Thin with a little anchovy oil. Finish with salt and pepper. At this point, taste and adjust seasonings, blending in a little more vinegar, if desired.

Serve over romaine lettuce leaves with a generous helping of croutons.

1 small yellow onion,
    peeled and cut into wedges
1 to 1^1/$_2$ heads elephant garlic, peeled,
    or 4 cloves regular garlic
2 to 4 canned anchovy fillets,
    packing oil reserved
^{1}/$_3$ cup Dijon mustard
^{1}/$_4$ cup fresh lemon juice
2 teaspoons Worcestershire sauce
2 teaspoons hot pepper sauce,
    such as Tabasco
Equivalent of 12 egg yolks, pasteurized
2 to 3 teaspoons vinegar
1 quart olive oil
1 tablespoon salt
1 tablespoon pepper

Cook's Tip: Elephant garlic is named for its enormous size. Despite their size, the large cloves of elephant garlic are much milder than their smaller cousin—perhaps because it is not true garlic, but rather a form of leek—so if you choose regular garlic over elephant garlic, use less and adjust for taste accordingly.

Grilled Tomato Vinaigrette

Despite the extra step of roasting or grilling the tomatoes in this recipe, this is a great salad dressing and worth the effort. My family couldn't get enough of it.

MAKES ABOUT 1$\frac{1}{2}$ QUARTS

Brush tomato halves with olive oil. Place face down on baking sheet and season with salt and pepper. Place under broiler for 5 minutes or until soft and lightly charred. Do not peel. (Can prepare tomatoes on a hot grill instead, if desired.)

Remove tomatoes from heat. Using a spatula, transfer tomatoes to a bowl and chill in refrigerator for at least an hour.

In a blender or food processor, puree chilled tomatoes and remaining ingredients except the oil and Parmesan. While machine is running, slowly drizzle in the oil until fully emulsified.

6 Roma tomatoes, halved and seeded
Olive oil
Salt and pepper
2 tablespoons minced garlic
1 scant cup red wine vinegar
$\frac{1}{4}$ cup fresh lemon juice
1 teaspoon salt
1 teaspoon pepper
1 tablespoon Dijon mustard
1 tablespoon sugar
$\frac{1}{4}$ teaspoon oregano
1$\frac{1}{2}$ cups vegetable oil
$\frac{1}{2}$ cup grated Parmesan

Add Parmesan, salt, and pepper until blended.

Chill overnight. Use as a salad dressing over mixed greens or baby spinach. Will keep refrigerated for 2 days.

Breads & Brunch

Lemon Pepper Focaccia

Pomodoro was an Italian restaurant that restaurateur Kevin Taylor was involved with. His focaccia is infused with the tartness and flavor of lemon.

SERVES 6

Mix yeast in warm water and let stand for about 5 minutes, until yeast is completely dissolved. Stir together bread flour and pinch of salt in a large mixing bowl, add yeast mixture, and combine. Flour a work surface lightly, flour your hands, and knead dough for 10 minutes. Allow to rest uncovered for 10 minutes.

Roll out dough on a lightly floured surface to a 14-inch circle of $^{1}/_{2}$-inch thickness. Transfer the dough to an oiled baking sheet, such as a pizza pan, and brush heavily with olive oil. Sprinkle with the rosemary and a generous amount of pepper. Place lemon slices evenly over bread. Cover with a damp cloth and allow to rise 20 to 25 minutes in a warm area.

Preheat oven to 425 degrees.

With fingers spread apart, lightly make indentations in the bread—this allows the olive oil to stay in place. Bake 15 to 20 minutes or until

1 packet active dry yeast ($^{1}/_{4}$ ounce)
$^{3}/_{4}$ cup lukewarm (110 to 115 degrees) water
$1^{1}/_{2}$ cups bread flour
Pinch of salt
$^{1}/_{2}$ cup virgin olive oil
1 tablespoon chopped fresh rosemary
Freshly ground pepper
$^{1}/_{2}$ lemon, thinly sliced and seeded
2 tablespoons grated Parmesan

golden brown. Remove from the oven and brush heavily with more olive oil. Sprinkle with Parmesan.

Note: It's best to use bread flour rather than all-purpose flour, because its higher protein content aids in keeping the dough from deflating.

Cook's Tip: Focaccia is a flat, dimpled bread that's even being used for sandwiches these days. You can experiment with other toppings if lemon isn't for you. Think of the focaccia as a canvas for other toppings, just as with Boboli or pizza dough. I spread olive oil, pureed garlic, and Parmesan on top. This recipe can be ready in the time it takes you to make the rest of your meal.

Sour Cherry Oat Bran Muffins

This recipe is from Fred Bramhall, owner of Bluepoint Bakery, which supplies many of the baked goods and breads at Denver area restaurants. The muffins were originally sold at Pour la France. The muffins look and taste just like a muffin that you would expect to buy at a bakery—large and delicious—even though they are made with a healthful combination of wheat bran, oat bran, and rolled oats. In order to reduce this from a huge bakery batch into one that would fit into my electric mixer, I ended up with some odd measurements. Note that the batter is very dense.

MAKES 1 DOZEN JUMBO MUFFINS

Cream butter, sugars, baking powder, and salt. Mix in egg whites gradually; scrape sides of mixing bowl and add applesauce. Add dry ingredients and stir just to blend. Stir in cherries. Fill greased muffin tins to the top and bake at 375 degrees until set (approximately 30 minutes).

10$^1/_2$ ounces butter
(a little more than 2$^1/_2$ sticks), softened
1 cup packed brown sugar
$^5/_8$ cup sugar
1 tablespoon baking powder
$^1/_2$ teaspoon salt
$^3/_4$ cup egg whites (about 6 eggs)
10$^1/_2$ ounces applesauce
2$^1/_8$ cups oat bran
2$^5/_8$ cups all-purpose flour
1$^5/_8$ cups rolled oats
1$^3/_8$ cups wheat bran
1 pound sour cherries,
canned and drained, or frozen

Cook's Tip: *You'll need Texas-size muffin pans (the extra-large size) for these. Unlike a lot of muffin recipes where you only fill the tin half full, you'll want to fill the tins to the top because the batter doesn't rise much and is dense and moist.*

Apricot-Glazed Hot Cross Buns

Chef/owner Michael Bortz, formerly of Palmetto Grille, makes these hot cross buns for Easter. The dough is easy to make, especially for a yeast bread. The dough needs to rise twice which takes about an hour, but with a little planning, the buns can be ready to serve right out of the oven at a brunch.

MAKES 1 DOZEN BUNS

To make buns: Dissolve sugar and yeast in milk and let sit for about 5 minutes or until yeast is completely dissolved. Add salt, butter, eggs, lemon zest, and spices to milk mixture and mix. Gradually add flour, mix, and knead until you have a smooth dough: 6 to 7 minutes by hand (be sure to flour hands so that dough doesn't stick), 6 to 8 minutes with a dough hook. Knead in fruit.

Place dough in lightly greased bowl and cover with plastic wrap. Let sit in warm place until doubled, about 30 minutes. Punch down dough. On an unfloured counter, work dough into a loaf shape and roll by hand into an 18-inch long roll. Cut into 12 pieces about

1/4 cup sugar
2 packets dry active yeast (1/4 ounce each)
1 cup lukewarm (110 to 115 degrees) milk
1 teaspoon salt
3 tablespoons melted butter, cooled
2 eggs, beaten lightly
2 teaspoons fresh lemon zest
Pinch of cinnamon
Pinch of nutmeg
4 cups all-purpose flour
1/4 cup candied fruit, raisins, or currants
1 cup apricot marmalade
1/2 cup water
1/2 cup sifted confectioners' sugar
Water

1 1/2 inches thick each; then roll each piece into balls between the palms of your hands. Place in 8- or 9-inch round pans, about 6 per pan, leaving space between them for rolls to expand during rising. Let double again, about 30 minutes. Bake at 350 degrees for 15 to 20 minutes.

(continued on next page)

Place marmalade and water in a small saucepan and bring to a boil. Strain through a fine sieve. While buns are still hot, brush glaze liberally over them with a pastry brush.

Mix confectioners' sugar with enough water to make a smooth spreadable paste. Place in pastry bag and pipe a thin, steady stream across rolls in an X pattern. (Be sure that rolls have completely cooled so that the Xs won't run.)

· ·

Brown Palace Scones

The Brown Palace is famous for its elegant formal teas, held everyday in the lobby of the historic Denver hotel. The scones are as famous as the hotel's macaroons. They're cut in rounds instead of traditional wedges and served with clotted cream, also known as Devonshire cream (available in some groceries and in most specialty food stores).

MAKES 18 SCONES

Mix flour and baking powder in a bowl. Cut butter into flour mixture with pastry blender or two knives, until mixture resembles coarse cornmeal. Add the sugar, eggs, and buttermilk and blend with a fork, just until mixture adheres. Do not overmix. Chill in bowl for at least 1 hour.

Preheat oven to 375 degrees.

Roll out chilled dough on lightly floured surface to $1/2$-inch thickness. Using a biscuit cutter

3 cups flour
1 tablespoon baking powder
5 tablespoons chilled butter
$1/3$ cup sugar
3 eggs, beaten lightly
$3/4$ cup buttermilk
Egg wash (whisk together one egg
    plus 1 tablespoon water)

or the floured rim of a drinking glass, cut $2^1/2$-inch circles. Brush tops of scones with egg wash (this gives the tops a glossy look after they bake). Place scones on parchment-lined baking sheet. Bake for 15 minutes or until golden brown.

Cook's Tip: Parchment paper is available at groceries or kitchenware stores. Lining the baking sheets will make it easier to remove the scones.

Banana Bread French Toast

This vegetarian restaurant serves some delicious meatless meals. Although I couldn't persuade restaurant owner Dan Landes to part with its gravy recipe, which is high on our request list, he was willing to share this recipe for Banana Bread French Toast. (You can also eat the banana bread without turning it into french toast.)

MAKES 8 SLICES

Preheat oven to 350 degrees.

Sift flours, baking powder, sea salt, and baking soda. In a separate bowl, mash bananas with lemon juice. Cream butter and brown sugar; mix with mashed banana mixture. Stir in flour mixture and mix until blended.

Pour batter in a 9 × 5-inch greased loaf pan and bake for 45 to 50 minutes. Turn loaf out of pan onto a wire rack and let cool.

After loaf has cooled, combine eggs, soy milk, and vanilla and whisk together.

$^3/_4$ cup whole wheat flour
$^3/_4$ cup white flour
$^1/_2$ teaspoon baking powder
$^1/_2$ teaspoon sea salt
$^1/_2$ teaspoon baking soda
4 ripe bananas
$1^1/_2$ tablespoons fresh lemon juice
$^3/_4$ cup butter, softened
$^3/_4$ cup packed brown sugar
2 eggs
$^1/_4$ cup Vitasoy soy milk
1 tablespoon pure vanilla extract

Slice banana bread into 1-inch-thick slices and dip each in egg mixture, coating both sides. Brown on each side in a skillet over medium-high heat. Top with honey-roasted walnuts and syrup, if desired.

Buttermilk Biscuits with Honey Butter

This is really a delicious biscuit recipe, with or without the honey butter. Noted cooking expert Marion Cunningham calls biscuits the "little black dress of baking," because they're always appropriate for any kind of meal.

MAKES ABOUT 1 DOZEN BISCUITS

Preheat oven to 450 degrees.

Cut butter into cubes. Put all dry ingredients in bowl of food processor, add cubed butter, and pulse until butter is pea-sized. Do not overmix. Add buttermilk; mix until just incorporated. Once mixed, place dough on a lightly floured surface and roll out to $3/4$-inch thick and cut into rounds with a floured biscuit cutter. Bake for 12 to 15 minutes on a nonstick cookie sheet. Serve hot.

$2^1/2$ cups all-purpose flour
$1/2$ pound (2 sticks) chilled unsalted butter
$1/8$ cup sugar
1 teaspoon baking powder
$3/4$ teaspoon salt
1 cup buttermilk
1 stick unsalted butter, softened at room temperature
Clover honey to taste

Place the softened butter in a mixing bowl and whip with an electric mixer until the butter looks light and fluffy. Reduce the speed of the mixer and add the honey, one tablespoon at a time, until it has the desired sweetness.

Serve honey butter with hot buttermilk biscuits.

Carrot Spice Bread

When Palmetto Grille was open, chef/owner Michael Bortz would place a basket of bread on the table that included this carrot spice bread (which a lot of people thought was pumpkin bread). Bortz is now the corporate baker for Paradise Bakery.

MAKES 2 9 × 5-INCH LOAVES

Preheat oven to 325 degrees.

Combine flour with baking powder, baking soda, salt, and spices and mix together.

In an electric mixer or bowl, place eggs, mayonnaise, and sugars and mix to combine. Add flour mixture and carrot and mix to combine. Fold in raisins by hand. Grease 2 loaf pans and pour even amounts of batter into each.

Bake for 60 to 70 minutes, covering with foil midway through the baking if bread gets too browned on top.

This bread tastes best if allowed to rest overnight. Cool, cover tightly with foil. Can be frozen.

4 cups flour
$1^1/2$ teaspoons baking powder
$1/2$ teaspoon baking soda
$1^1/4$ teaspoons salt
1 tablespoon cinnamon
1 teaspoon nutmeg
$1/4$ teaspoon allspice
$1/4$ teaspoon ginger
6 eggs
2 cups mayonnaise
$2^1/2$ cups packed brown sugar
1 cup white sugar
$1/2$ cup grated carrot
$1/2$ cup raisins (optional)

Cook's Tip: *Yes, the ingredient amounts, including the 2 cups of mayonnaise, are correct.*

Swiss Fruit Bread and Breakfast "Salad"

This breakfast "salad" calls for granola, yogurt, and a fruit bread. The fruit bread is a delicious combination of apples, dates (don't worry non-date lovers, you can't taste them), raisins, and bananas, but it really tastes more like a banana bread than anything else.

SERVES 6 TO 8

Preheat oven to 350 degrees.

Grease and flour 2 large (9 × 5 × 3-inch) loaf pans. Mix dry ingredients. (The amount of baking powder is correct.) Add oil and milk; mix. Add eggs and blend until smooth. Stir in fruit and walnuts and mix.

Pour batter into the loaf pans, filling each no more than half to two-thirds full.

Bake for 50 minutes to 1 hour. (Cover lightly with foil midway through baking if breads appear to be browning too fast on top.) Test for doneness with a toothpick. (When inserted in center of loaf, toothpick should come out clean.)

4 cups all-purpose flour
$1^1/_2$ cups sugar
4 teaspoons baking powder
$1^1/_2$ teaspoons salt
$^2/_3$ cup oil
1 cup milk
3 large eggs
1 cup mashed banana (2 or 3)
$^1/_2$ cup diced peeled apple (1 small)
$^1/_3$ cup raisins or golden raisins
$^1/_3$ cup chopped dates
1 cup crushed walnuts
Fruit and Honey Yogurt
   (see recipe that follows)
Granola, commercial or homemade

Serve the Fruit and Honey Yogurt with your favorite granola (about 3 ounces per person) and warmed slices of Swiss Fruit Bread with softened cream cheese.

3 cups nonfat yogurt
1 cup frozen sliced strawberries (thawed)
$^1/_4$ cup honey

Fruit and Honey Yogurt

MAKES ABOUT $3^1/_2$ CUPS

Mix together yogurt, strawberries, and honey.

Pancakes

While I was making these pancakes for my family, I joked, "What happens when you substitute real pancakes for the pancake mix you usually use?" The answer is, they ask for more.

MAKES ABOUT 1 DOZEN
MEDIUM-SIZED PANCAKES

Sift flour before measuring, then sift again with other dry ingredients. In a separate bowl lightly beat the eggs and mix with the butter and vanilla. Quickly stir into the flour mixture and add enough milk so that the batter can easily be poured. Do not overmix. Batter will be slightly lumpy.

Spray griddle with a light coating of vegetable oil spray and heat until a few drops of water dropped on the griddle's surface bounce and sizzle. (If you're using a skillet, coat with a thin layer of vegetable oil.) Pour or ladle enough batter for one pancake onto the griddle. Use

$1^1/_2$ cups all-purpose flour
1 teaspoon salt
3 tablespoons sugar
$1^3/_4$ teaspoons baking powder
2 eggs
3 tablespoons melted butter, cooled
$^1/_2$ teaspoon vanilla
1 to $1^1/_4$ cups milk

the first pancake as a test for size and consistency. If batter seems too thick, add a little more milk. If too thin, add a little more flour. Turn the pancakes only once—when small bubbles appear in the batter and some begin to pop, and when you lift up the edge of the underside and it has browned. The second side won't take as long to cook. Serve pancakes with butter and warm maple syrup.

Panzanella

Panzanella, also known as Italian bread salad, is a good way to use up day-old bread. In fact, it's essential that the bread used in this salad be day-old and not standard sliced white bread—this keeps it from becoming soggy. This makes a nice addition to a breakfast buffet, but can be served at any meal.

SERVES 8

Cube and toast the bread. Toss all ingredients together and let sit for about 10 minutes to make sure flavors meld. Season with salt and pepper to taste. Serve immediately at room temperature (it's important to serve right away so bread won't be soggy).

$^1/_2$ pound day-old rustic or artisan bread, preferably whole wheat or combination
6 Roma tomatoes, each cut into sixths
6 large fresh basil leaves, rolled and julienned
$^1/_4$ small red onion, julienned
1 clove garlic, chopped
$^3/_4$ cup extra virgin olive oil
$^1/_4$ cup balsamic vinegar
Salt and pepper to taste

Willie's Special

Leo Goto of the Wellshire Inn used to own a restaurant downtown called Leo's Place. When a diner at the Wellshire Inn asked Leo if he could make her a Willie's Special from the good ol' days of Leo's Place, he served up this combination of spinach, scrambled eggs, and ground beef. The recipe may seem unusual, but it's Leo's take on the classic Joe's Special that originated in San Francisco.

SERVES 4

2 tablespoons olive oil
2 large cloves garlic
1 pound ground sirloin beef
8 handfuls fresh spinach leaves, washed and trimmed
4 to 6 large eggs, lightly beaten
2 tablespoons butter
Salt and pepper to taste

Heat large cast-iron or heavy skillet. Add olive oil and brown the whole garlic cloves; discard garlic when browned all over.

Add ground beef, stirring until browned and thoroughly cooked to 160 degrees. Throw in spinach leaves and mix thoroughly. Cover skillet and turn off heat, allowing spinach to steam. In a separate pan, scramble eggs in butter.

Salt and pepper spinach–ground beef mixture to taste. Divide into individual servings on warmed plates. Top with scrambled eggs and serve immediately.

Eggs Taos

The Eggs Taos dish of Marina Landing is still served at the Bull and Bush. The secret ingredients: cream cheese in the scrambled eggs and green chili with pork, the latter of which you can buy at the Bull and Bush for use at home. You might also use the Green Chili recipe in this book (see page 46). Or use one of the prepared varieties found on the grocery shelves. This is a wonderful recipe, easy enough to whip up just before company arrives.

MAKES 1 9 × 13-INCH CASSEROLE

Beat eggs with milk in a small bowl. Melt 4 tablespoons butter in skillet. Pour in eggs. When slightly set, add cream cheese. Scramble to desired consistency. Lay tortillas flat. Divide egg mixture among tortillas, placing egg mixture down the middle of each tortilla.

Preheat oven to 400 degrees.

Place slices of avocado on top of eggs. Cover egg and avocado with a few teaspoons of green chili. Fold tortillas as you would burritos. Place in baking dish. Smother tortillas with remaining green chili. Sprinkle cheese over top. Place in oven 5 to 10 minutes or until cheese is melted and dish is heated through.

10 eggs
1/4 cup milk
4 tablespoons butter
6 ounces cream cheese, cut in cubes
5 tortillas
2 avocados
1 15-ounce can green chili with pork
2 cups shredded marbled Cheddar cheese
   (or more, to taste)
Salsa (optional)

Cook's Tip: *You can substitute a product such as Stokes Green Chili with Chicken, if desired, without changing the flavor of the recipe. The casserole should serve at least 8, depending on how many other dishes you are serving.*

Haystack Mountain Goat Cheese and Mushroom Omelet

Chef/owner Bradford Heap is a busy guy, splitting his time between Chautauqua Dining Hall and Full Moon Grill in Boulder. I enjoyed this omelet one sunny afternoon while dining on the veranda at Chautauqua, but it's easy to recreate at home for that special someone (just reduce the ingredients by half).

MAKES 4 OMELETS

Melt 2 tablespoons of butter in a skillet; add mushrooms and sauté until translucent. When mushrooms are half-cooked, add onion and cook just until the juices are released (mushrooms contain a lot of liquid).

Crack eggs (3 per omelet) in a bowl and whip lightly; season with salt and pepper and add cream.

In another pan—a broiler-proof skillet—add 1 tablespoon butter. When butter foams, add a quarter of the egg mixture to the pan and cook over medium heat, swirling eggs with a heat-proof rubber spatula and shaking pan vigorously until they're thickened but still soft. (Do not allow eggs to brown.)

> 6 tablespoons butter
> 1 cup chopped button, shiitake, or
>   portobello mushrooms
> 1/2 onion, chopped
> 12 eggs
> Salt and pepper to taste
> 3 tablespoons cream
> 1/2 cup crumbled Haystack Mountain
>   Goat Cheese

When eggs are almost cooked, add a quarter of the mushroom mixture, sprinkling with cheese on top; finish cooking eggs and melting cheese under a broiler.

Repeat process to make the rest of the omelets.

Cook's Tips: Use a small skillet that's the exact size you want the omelet to be, and dispense with the flipping business. (I know, I know, it's a frittata, not an omelet, but if it looks like a duck …) Also, don't overbrown the eggs; rather, add the cheese when the omelet is almost cooked and run the whole thing under the broiler.

Breakfast Torte

Dishes from the Wellshire Inn are among the most frequently requested. I love this torte. It's showier than an omelet but with a similar flavor profile.

MAKES 1 10-INCH TORTE

Soft scramble 8 eggs. In a 10-inch round pan (3 inches high), form one layer of puff pastry dough, shaping the edges to fit. On top of this, layer half of the scrambled egg mixture. Next, layer vegetables, forming separate layers for each to create definite color strata. Place remaining eggs over last layer. Cover with cheese and fold second layer of dough on top.

Lightly beat reserved egg. Brush dough with the reserved egg to give an even brown sheen to the pastry top as it bakes.

Bake at 350 degrees for 1 hour. (After 45 minutes, check pie by inserting sharp knife in the middle; filling should be firm not watery.)

8 large eggs, plus
   1 for brushing dough before baking
2 sheets frozen puff pastry dough,
   thawed according to package directions
1 pound mushrooms, sliced and
   cooked with salt and juice of $1/2$ lemon
1 large roasted red bell pepper,
   skinned and julienned
1 pound spinach, cooked with $1/4$ cup
   grated onion and a sprinkle of nutmeg
   just until soft (drain well after cooking)
1 bunch asparagus, with ends broken off,
   cut into 1-inch pieces diagonally,
   and poached
8 ounces sliced Swiss cheese

Cook's Tip: I used what I like in an omelet, such as sautéed onions, sautéed mushrooms, and spinach, and left out the bell pepper and asparagus. Use whatever you like, and use any cheese you like, including shredded Monterey or Colby Jack. Pepperidge Farms makes the puff pastry—you'll find it in the freezer aisle of the grocery store.

Eggplant Sandwich with Orzo Salad

The ingredients for the actual sandwich are simple—eggplant, red onion, beefsteak tomatoes, focaccia, Ricotta Spread, Balsamic Vinaigrette. Note, however, that you cook the onions in balsamic vinegar for 45 minutes—that's essential to the success of the sandwich. Also, the Orzo Salad should be made an hour before serving, so plan ahead.

MAKES 6 SANDWICHES

Cut the red onion into ¹/₂-inch-thick slices and simmer in balsamic vinegar for 45 minutes. The onions will caramelize, making them soft and sweet; they will absorb a lot of the vinegar. Set aside.

Brush sliced eggplant with Balsamic Vinaigrette, salt, and pepper and grill or broil until golden brown (about 7 minutes per side; brush with oil again when you turn eggplant). Cut beefsteak tomatoes into thick slices, brush with oil, and grill or broil for 3 minutes.

Balsamic Vinaigrette

MAKES 1 CUP

Whisk together all ingredients.

1 red onion
Balsamic vinegar, to cover onions
1 large eggplant, sliced
Balsamic Vinaigrette
   (see recipe that follows)
Salt and pepper to taste
2 beefsteak tomatoes
Focaccia (can be bought sliced
   at specialty grocery stores)
Ricotta Spread (see recipe that follows)
Orzo Salad (see recipe that follows)

Toast focaccia, apply Ricotta Spread and build sandwich with grilled eggplant and tomato. Top with the balsamic onions. Serve open faced. Drizzle a small amount of the vinaigrette over top of sandwich. Serve sandwich with Orzo Salad.

¹/₂ shallot, minced
1 clove garlic, minced
¹/₄ cup balsamic vinegar
³/₄ cup olive oil

Ricotta Spread

MAKES 1 CUP

Mix ricotta with remaining ingredients. Refrigerate until use.

1 cup ricotta
3 green onions, finely diced
6 sun-dried tomatoes (rehydrate and dice)
6 to 8 fresh basil leaves, finely chopped

Orzo Salad

MAKES 6 CUPS

Whisk together all ingredients, except pasta. Toss with cooked pasta. Cover and refrigerate for at least 1 hour before serving so that flavors will meld.

Cook's Tip: Orzo is a tiny, rice-shaped pasta, found at any grocery, that in our never-to-be-humble opinion is underutilized. It lends texture to lots of different flavor combinations, and could be combined with shredded cooked chicken or diced ham and just about any vegetables, for a stand-alone main dish, light lunch, or salad.

2 tablespoons minced garlic
1/4 cup chopped fresh basil
1/4 cup chopped fresh oregano
1 cup sun-dried tomatoes, rehydrated and chopped (or use 1 8$1/2$-ounce jar of sun-dried tomatoes in oil, drained)
1 cup chopped scallions or green onions
1 cup cubed feta cheese
1/4 cup fresh lemon juice
1/4 cup soy sauce
1/2 cup olive oil
1 pound orzo (rice-shaped pasta), cooked

Basil Lemonade

Basil lemonade? Hard to believe, but this refreshing beverage from Epicurean Catering will wow them at your next summertime event. Nectarines and basil are combined with prepared lemonade for an interesting twist on a classic.

MAKES ABOUT 4 QUARTS

In a large pot, add the water, basil, nectarines, and sugar. Cooking over medium heat, reduce liquid by half; strain and chill. When ready to serve, add lemonade and ice cubes.

4 quarts water
$1/4$ pound fresh basil, chopped
6 nectarines, pitted and diced
6 tablespoons sugar
2 quarts prepared lemonade
Ice cubes

Cook's Tip: If you prefer your lemonade tart, decrease the amount of sugar.

Entrees

(continued on next page)

Entrees, *continued*

Almond-Encrusted Chicken with Cranberry and Cream Sauce   118

Sesame Chicken   120

Chicken and Penne with Roasted Chile Sauce   121

Chicken with Anasazi Mix and Chipotle Cream Sauce   123

Anasazi Chicken Enchiladas   125

Salisbury Steak, Palace Arms–Style

Salisbury steak was a specialty item of the Brown Palace Hotel in the past. It shows up on the menu as a special from time to time. The original nineteenth-century version was made with ground beef.

SERVES 4

In a large, cast-iron skillet over high heat, sear the steaks for one minute per side in the olive oil. Remove them from the pan. Briefly sauté the mushrooms, garlic, and shallots. Deglaze the pan with the red wine, and add the thyme. Add in demi-glace and the steaks. Bring to a simmer for 10 to 12 minutes, until the steaks are cooked through. Gently stir the truffle oil into the sauce just prior to serving.

Cook's Tips: *Cubed steak, also called minute steak, is available at the meat counter. It's a tough cut of meat from the round that the butcher has tenderized by running through a machine twice to break up the muscle tissue.*

4 10-ounce cubed steaks
1/4 cup olive oil
1 cup sliced mushrooms
1 cup sliced shiitake mushrooms
1/8 cup finely minced garlic
1/4 cup finely minced shallots
1/2 cup red wine
2 tablespoons chopped fresh thyme
4 cups demi-glace
2 teaspoons truffle oil

Demi-glace is a rich, reduced beef stock and is available at specialty groceries. Truffle oil, also available at specialty stores, adds some extra flavor to the sauce. Be sure that when you buy the oil, you check for freshness (an expiration date should appear on the bottle). The oil's potency only lasts about a year; opened bottles should be stored in the refrigerator for no longer than 3 months. Although this oil is too delicate to cook with, it is delicious drizzled on salads, pasta, vegetables, and seafood.

Short Ribs of Beef

Short ribs have become a popular comfort food lately, despite their rather high price tag. These are delicious —and the sauce would be tasty over mashed potatoes.

SERVES 3 TO 4

Brown short ribs in oil in a heavy pan. Remove. Deglaze pan with the red wine, scraping up any browned bits. Add shallots, garlic, carrot, onion, and celery; continue cooking for 10 minutes. Add beef stock, tomato paste, and pepper.

Place short ribs and sauce into a braising pan (a heavy lidded pot or dutch oven), cover tightly, and cook in oven at 300 degrees for 3 to 3 1/2 hours until tender.

Remove short ribs and strain pan liquid through sieve. Make a roux for thickening the sauce by whisking together flour and butter in a saucepan over medium heat. When roux is golden brown and bubbling, add 2 cups of the hot strained liquid, whisking until blended and thickened. (Add more liquid, if need be, to get desired consistency.) You may also add horseradish to the finished sauce to give it additional punch.

12 beef short ribs
2 tablespoons oil
1 cup red wine
4 shallots, minced
4 cloves garlic, minced
1 carrot, peeled and diced
1 onion, diced
4 stalks celery, diced
1 1/2 quarts rich beef stock
1 6-ounce can tomato paste
1 tablespoon cracked pepper
4 tablespoons flour
4 tablespoons butter
1/4 cup prepared horseradish (optional)

Cook's Tip: Note that these short ribs need 3 or more hours to cook, so plan ahead. They reheat well; make them a day ahead and refrigerate, and you'll have dinner ready to go.

Beef Stroganoff

The request for this recipe came with a note asking about the secret ingredient that the diner couldn't identify. No wonder. Executive Chef Cruz Imaz says it's sweet pickle relish.

SERVES 4

Warm a covered casserole dish in the oven.

Slice beef into thin strips, about 1 inch wide by 2 inches long. Dredge strips in seasoned flour and shake off excess.

Melt butter in a large, heavy skillet over medium heat; add the meat and sauté until medium done. Add onions and mushrooms and sauté for a few minutes more until onions are tender but not browned.

Add the sherry and beef broth, scraping the bottom of the pan thoroughly until all residue is dissolved and alcohol has evaporated. Stir in sour cream, tomato puree, and sweet pickle relish; mix to incorporate and heat through.

Prepare noodles al dente according to package directions. Drain, drizzle with olive oil, and add a small pinch of nutmeg. Toss.

1 1/4 pounds beef tenderloin
1 cup flour, seasoned with salt and pepper
1/2 stick butter (1/4 cup)
1/3 cup finely diced onions
1 cup sliced fresh mushrooms
1/4 cup dry sherry
1/4 cup beef broth
1 1/2 cups sour cream
4 teaspoons tomato puree
2 teaspoons sweet pickle relish
Salt and pepper to taste
8 ounces wide egg noodles
Olive oil
Pinch of ground nutmeg

Fold noodles into beef mixture in the skillet and season with salt and pepper. When thoroughly incorporated, pour mixture into warmed casserole dish and serve immediately.

Fat Tire Ribeye Steaks

This recipe includes a Sweet Soy Glaze that is part of the marinade for the steaks and is also drizzled on the cooked steaks at the end. You'll want to make the glaze first.

SERVES 4

Combine all ingredients except olive oil and meat in food processor or blender; blend. While blending, add oil in a small stream to create an emulsion.

Pour mixture over steaks. Cover and refrigerate for at least 4 hours. Discard marinade and grill the steaks to desired doneness.

$1/4$ cup minced garlic
$1/4$ cup minced fresh cilantro
$1/4$ cup minced fresh parsley
1 tablespoon chopped fresh oregano
3 tablespoons Worcestershire sauce
1 bottle Fat Tire beer
$1/2$ cup Sweet Soy Glaze (see recipe that follows; reserve remaining glaze)
1 cup olive oil
4 ribeye steaks

Drizzle remaining Sweet Soy Glaze over grilled steaks and serve.

Sweet Soy Glaze

MAKES $1^3/4$ CUPS

Combine all ingredients for glaze except soy sauce in a small pot and heat to boiling. Keep boiling mixture for 10 to 15 minutes until all sugar granules are melted and mixture begins to look like clear corn syrup.

1 cup sugar
$1/3$ cups water
1 tablespoon fresh lemon juice
$1/2$ cup soy sauce

Remove from stove and refrigerate the mixture until temperature lowers to about 125 degrees (use a food thermometer and be extra careful when handling hot sugar), which takes about 15 minutes. Stir in soy sauce.

Steak au Poivre with Dijon Sauce

The Hearthstone is in a historic, 100-year-old Victorian house in Breckenridge. Although steak au poivre is traditionally made with a New York strip steak, this recipe calls for filet mignon. The sauce would also be good over chicken and pasta.

SERVES 4

Spread cracked pepper on a plate. Press both sides of steaks into the pepper.

Off the heat, pour brandy into a heavy 2-quart saucepan. Carefully heat brandy over very low heat, and simmer until reduced in volume by half. (Because of the brandy's volatility, do not use high heat; do not boil; do not leave stove unattended.) Add cream, mustard, and salt to the reduction, whisking together; bring to a boil. Continue cooking at a low boil, whisking occasionally, until sauce is reduced by about half. If you prefer a thicker sauce, reduce further.

Preheat oven to 400 degrees. Cook steaks to desired doneness. Serve with sauce over the top.

$1/4$ cup cracked pepper
4 thick filets mignons
$1/4$ cup brandy
$1^1/4$ cups heavy cream
1 tablespoon country-style Dijon mustard
$1/2$ teaspoon salt

Beef Tenderloin with Shiitake Marsala Demi-Glace and Potato Rosti and Asparagus Spears

The mushroom demi-glace in this recipe is delicious and elegant. Rosti potatoes are crisp, shredded potatoes in pancake form.

SERVES 4

To make the shiitake marsala demi-glace: Heat olive oil in saucepan over medium heat. Add the shiitake mushrooms and garlic. Sauté until soft but not browned. Add Marsala to pan and reduce until almost dry. Add demi-glace and heat through. Finish with butter, stirring until melted.

To make the potato rosti: Combine grated potatoes with julienned onions and steam for 5 to 7 minutes until soft (mixture will be very sticky and starchy). Season with salt.

Gather warm potato mixture into four 4-ounce portions and shape and press by hand into flat patties. (Making each portion very compact will aid in frying.) In a saucepan, heat oil to 350 degrees, cover the 4 potato rosti halfway. Cook until underside is golden brown; turn and brown other side.

2 tablespoons olive oil
20 fresh shiitake mushrooms, cleaned, stems removed
3 cloves garlic, slivered
1/4 cup marsala
12 ounces prepared demi-glace
2 tablespoons butter
3 russet potatoes, peeled and finely grated
1 yellow onion, julienned
Salt to taste
Vegetable oil for frying
Beef tenderloin fillets for 4
20 asparagus spears
Cracked pepper for garnish

To finish: Cook tenderloin at 400 degrees to desired doneness. Steam the asparagus spears while meat is cooking. To serve, place a potato rosti in center of each of 4 large plates. Place tenderloin on top of rosti. Place 5 asparagus spears around each steak and potato patty. Top whole thing with sauce. Garnish with cracked pepper.

Cook's Tip: *You can buy demi-glace at specialty food stores and some groceries, usually in a small tin (1.5 ounces). It's a reduced brown sauce made from veal and beef stock and red wine that chefs learn to make because it's more concentrated and flavorful than beef broth. The demi-glace is mixed with water the way you would with a bouillon cube. Demi-glace is also available frozen. Follow the instructions on the package for use.*

Roasted Pork Loin with Apple Chutney Sauce

Long-time chef Patrick Delaney has an apple chutney sauce that gives this dish its distinctive flavor. He was happy to provide the recipe for the home cook.

SERVES 4

Preheat oven to 400 degrees.

Mix all ingredients except pork loin and soy sauce in heavy non-aluminum saucepan, cover, and bring slowly to a boil. Uncover and simmer, stirring occasionally 1 to 1 1/2 hours until thick. Add brown sauce. Stir well to incorporate.

As sauce begins to cook, brush pork with soy sauce. Roast in oven for 35 to 40 minutes or until internal temperature registers 160 degrees.

Pull out of oven and let rest 1/2 hour before slicing into medallions. (Resting is critical, because it ensures that the meat's juices don't seep out, but instead are retained.)

Serve pork medallions with warm chutney sauce spooned over them.

3 large Granny Smith apples, peeled, cored, and coarsely chopped
1/2 cup seeded, minced red bell pepper
1/2 cup minced yellow onion
1/2 clove garlic, peeled and minced
1/2 pound seedless raisins
1/2 pound dark brown sugar
1 cup apple cider vinegar
1 1/2 teaspoons ground ginger
1 1/2 teaspoons ground cinnamon
1 teaspoon powdered English mustard
1 teaspoon salt
1/8 teaspoon dried, crushed red pepper flakes
1 cup brown sauce (commercial demi-glace or powdered brown)
2 pounds boneless pork loin
Low-sodium soy sauce

Veal Piccata

We frequently get requests for recipes from this Italian restaurant in Littleton. Owner Tommaso Candiano will make you feel like family.

SERVES 3 TO 4

Veal should be sliced or pounded almost paper-thin. Dust 2 veal slices, both sides, with flour. Bring large, nonstick sauté pan to medium-high heat. Add 2 tablespoons butter to pan until it melts; immediately add veal slices.

Add about a quarter of the sliced mushrooms to the pan and about a quarter of the chopped garlic. Squeeze one lemon wedge on each slice of veal. Add desired amount of capers to pan and a splash of caper juice on each slice. Finally, add about a quarter of the chopped parsley.

When the veal slices are gold in color on the underside, turn them over. Add $1/4$ cup of chicken broth. Salt and pepper the veal.

6 to 8 2-ounce thin veal slices
$1/2$ cup flour, on plate for dusting veal slices
$1/2$ pound butter (2 sticks or 16 tablespoons)
$1/2$ pound mushrooms, thinly sliced
1 to $1^1/2$ lemons, sliced into 6 to 8 wedges per lemon (one for each slice of veal)
Small jar of high-quality capers, drained (save the juice)
$1/4$ cup chopped fresh parsley
3 to 4 cloves garlic, chopped
1 cup chicken stock or broth
Salt and pepper to taste
1 cup dry white wine

Add $1/4$ cup of white wine to the pan. As the liquid in pan begins to bubble, add two pinches of the flour that remains from dusting the veal and stir. Reduce the liquid for about 30 seconds. Stop cooking when sauce starts to thicken.

(continued on next page)

Place finished veal slices in glass baking dish and scrape all sauce onto them. Place in warm oven to await next batch.

Flour next two veal slices and put 2 tablespoons butter in pan; when butter is melted, add veal and repeat entire process.

Cook's Tip: Use a meat mallet to flatten veal slices or ask the butcher to do it for you. Cook only two slices at a time; juice of capers provides flavor as veal cooks and adds acidity to this delicate dish—as does the lemon juice. Because these thin slices of veal cook very quickly, prepare ingredients before cooking so that they are ready and close at hand.

Braised Lamb Shank with Sauce Naturel

Braised lamb shanks became popular a few years ago as the ultimate in comfort food. Braising—which for meat means cooking slowly in liquid to tenderize it—is used in several recipes in this book. This technique also really brings out the flavors in foods.

SERVES 2

In large thick-bottomed pot, heat the olive oil. Season lamb shanks with salt and pepper, and sear in oil on all sides; then remove.

Add garlic, carrots, celery, and onions to pot; sauté until tender. Add tomato paste, mix well with the vegetables, and continue to sauté until they begin to brown.

Add red wine and simmer for 5 minutes.

Add stock, bay leaf, thyme, and rosemary and bring to a boil.

Add lamb shanks, making sure they are covered completely with liquid. Reduce heat and bring liquid to a simmer. Cover pot and simmer shanks until very tender, approximately $1^1/2$ to 2 hours.

4 ounces olive oil
4 lamb shanks
Dash salt and pepper
2 tablespoons minced garlic
1 cup diced carrots
1 cup diced celery
2 cups diced onions
$1/2$ cup tomato paste
3 cups red wine
1 quart lamb stock (may substitute beef broth)
1 bay leaf
1 sprig fresh thyme
1 sprig fresh rosemary

Remove shanks, strain liquid, pour liquid over shanks, and serve.

Cook's Tip: *Because this requires long, slow cooking, you'll want to plan ahead.*

Garlic Sausage Ragout with Peppery Saffron Polenta

This was a special one night at this popular restaurant, which specializes in pairing entrees with a choice of dipping sauces that run the flavor gamut from sweet to spicy.

SERVES 6 TO 8

In a non-aluminum saucepan over medium heat, reduce wine by half. (This will take about 45 minutes.) Heat a large stockpot over high heat, add olive oil, garlic, and shallots and sauté for 1 to 2 minutes. Add canned tomatoes, capers, sausage, and red wine reduction and cook for 15 minutes over medium heat. While this cooks, begin preparing polenta.

Add fresh tomato and basil and cook for an additional 10 minutes on medium heat. Season to taste with salt and pepper. Ladle ragout over polenta and serve.

1 bottle dry red wine
1/2 cup virgin olive oil
10 garlic cloves, thinly sliced—not chopped
6 shallots, thinly sliced—not chopped
1 14- to 16-ounce can peeled tomatoes
2 tablespoons capers, drained and rinsed
1 pound garlic sausage, cooked, cut in half lengthwise, and sliced (half-moon shapes)
Peppery Saffron Polenta
  (see recipe that follows)
8 ripe tomatoes, cut into 8 wedges each
1/2 cup chopped fresh basil
Kosher salt and
  freshly ground pepper to taste

Peppery Saffron Polenta

MAKES 2 CUPS

Bring the butter, half-and-half, chicken stock, saffron, and turmeric to a boil over high heat. Reduce heat to medium and slowly whisk in cornmeal by adding in steady stream. If corn starts to pull away from the sides of the pan, add more liquid (milk, stock, or water will all work) to create a creamy consistency. Add cracked peppercorns. Lower heat to medium low and cook for additional 5 to 8 minutes, stirring occasionally. If polenta is not creamy, add more liquid. Season to taste with kosher salt and additional butter.

1 stick butter (4 ounces or $1/2$ cup)
2 cups half-and-half
2 cups chicken stock
1 large pinch saffron
1 teaspoon turmeric
2 cups cornmeal
3 tablespoons cracked peppercorns
Kosher salt and additional butter to taste

Wazee Street Meat Loaf

Although known for its seafood, McCormick's can also serve up a very tasty meat loaf. This is similar to Pearl Street Grill's meat loaf, but uses a combination of ground pork and ground beef instead of ground chuck.

SERVES 8 TO 10

Preheat oven to 350 degrees.

Blend all ingredients well, mixing together with your hands (it's messy, but the best way to blend ingredients evenly). Place in one large or two smaller loaf pans, sprayed with an aerosol grease such as Pam. Press firmly into pan to form loaf.

Bake until internal temperature of 160 degrees is reached. It will take between 60 and 90 minutes (but start checking at 45 minutes, using a meat thermometer).

Let stand for 15 minutes; save juices and pan drippings for gravy.

$2^{1}/_{2}$ pounds ground beef
1 pound ground pork
$^{1}/_{8}$ cup pureed (or minced) mushroom
$^{1}/_{3}$ cup pureed (or minced) onion
$^{1}/_{4}$ cup ketchup
2 eggs
2 teaspoons pureed (or minced) garlic
2 teaspoons Worcestershire sauce
1 cup bread crumbs
1 teaspoon each salt and pepper

Pearl Street Grill Meat Loaf

3 pounds ground chuck
1 small yellow onion, diced
10 saltine crackers, crushed
1/2 cup ketchup
2 large eggs
1 teaspoon salt
1 to 2 teaspoons pepper or to taste
1 to 2 tablespoons Worcestershire sauce
Burgundy Sauce (see recipe that follows)

For their industrial-strength meat loaf recipe, the folks at Pearl Street Grill use 10 pounds of ground chuck, 1 1/4 cups ketchup, and 7 eggs. We've cut it down to a more manageable size.

SERVES 8 TO 10

Preheat oven to 350 degrees.

Mix together all ingredients (except Burgundy Sauce) by hand in large bowl and put mixture into a baking dish that's 8 inches square and 2 inches deep. Bake for 60 to 90 minutes or until meat loaf's internal temperature is 160 degrees when tested with a meat thermometer. Remove from oven and let rest for about 15 minutes. Serve with sauce.

Burgundy Sauce

MAKES 1 1/2 CUPS

Bring stock to a boil. Whisk in cornstarch and water mixture. Cook, reducing by half. Add wine, mushrooms, and pepper, and bring to boil again. Cook 5 minutes until thickened. If sauce tastes unbalanced, whisk a little bouillon into the pot and adjust seasonings. You can also add a couple pats of butter to flavor the sauce, if desired.

1 1/2 cups beef stock
1 tablespoon cornstarch, mixed with 1 tablespoon water
1 cup burgundy
Pinch cracked pepper
1/2 cup sliced mushrooms
Beef bouillon (optional)
Butter (optional)

Buffalo Meat Loaf with Chipotle Ketchup and Poblano Chile Sauce and Mashed Potatoes

This meat loaf is so good, it makes my mouth water just writing about it. Don't leave out the Poblano Chile Sauce or the Chipotle Ketchup. Once you've assembled everything and done the prep work, this combo comes together quickly.

SERVES 8 TO 10

Preheat oven to 325 degrees.

In a large mixing bowl combine all the meat, including the bacon, by hand, or mix with large electric mixer. Add the oats, vegetables, eggs, and spices; mix well. (For extra-spicy meat loaf, add red chili flakes.)

Place mixture into two small glass loaf pans and bake for 60 to 90 minutes. Meat thermometer should register 160 degrees when placed in center of loaves.

When meat loaf is done, brush the tops of the loaves with the Chipotle Ketchup and place loaves under the broiler until sauce starts to brown. (Save leftover ketchup for serving.) Remove loaves from oven and let rest for 10 to 15 minutes. Slice the meat loaf and arrange

1 pound ground buffalo or venison
$1/2$ pound ground pork
$1/2$ pound ground beef
6 strips applewood-smoked bacon, finely chopped
1 yellow onion, finely diced
1 carrot, finely diced
2 ribs celery, finely diced
1 poblano chile, seeded and finely diced
2 eggs, lightly beaten
1 cup uncooked oatmeal (do not use instant)
1 pinch ground cumin
1 pinch oregano
2 pinches paprika
1 pinch chili powder
1 teaspoon ground caraway seeds or $1/2$ teaspoon whole seeds
1 teaspon each salt and pepper
2 pinches red chili flakes (optional)
Chipotle Ketchup (see recipe that follows)
Poblano Chile Sauce (see recipe that follows)
Mel's Mashed Potatoes (see recipe that follows)

slices on individual serving plates. Spoon reserved ketchup on top. Pool Poblano Chile

Sauce around the meat loaf. Serve with mashed potatoes on the side.

Chipotle Ketchup

MAKES 1 CUP

Combine ketchup and chipotle chile to taste. Set aside.

1 cup ketchup
$1/4$ teaspoon chipotle chile powder
   or 2 to 3 pinches dried chipotle chile,
   or more to taste

Poblano Chile Sauce

MAKES 4 CUPS

Heat butter in medium saucepan. Add onion, garlic, shallot, red bell pepper, poblano chile, and corn; sauté until softened. Add chopped cilantro, turmeric, and heavy cream and bring just to the boil. Lower heat and cook on low until thick, about 20 minutes. Add the fresh lime juice and salt and pepper to taste.

2 tablespoons butter
$1/2$ yellow onion, finely diced
1 tablespoon minced garlic
1 tablespoon minced shallot
1 red bell pepper, seeded and finely diced
1 poblano chile, seeded and finely diced
2 ears fresh corn, kernels cut off cob
1 bunch cilantro, finely chopped
$1/2$ teaspoon turmeric
4 cups heavy cream
Juice of 1 lime
Salt and pepper to taste

(continued on next page)

Mel's Mashed Potatoes

Cover potatoes with cold water, add salt, and bring to a boil. Cook potatoes until soft. Drain water. Mash potatoes with buttermilk and butter—for chunkier potatoes, mash by hand, or for creamier potatoes, use an electric mixer. Season to taste with salt and white pepper.

6 large russet potatoes, peeled and cut in large chunks
Water for cooking
1 teaspoon salt
2^1/$_2$ to 3 cups buttermilk
1 stick butter (^{1}/$_4$ pound or ^{1}/$_2$ cup)
Salt and white pepper to taste

Chicken Piccata

Using chicken instead of the traditional veal in a piccata recipe is a good way to save money—though the texture is slightly different.

SERVES 2 TO 3

Dust chicken breasts in flour on both sides. Heat olive oil in sauté pan on medium-high heat. Add garlic, onion, and chicken breasts and cook chicken through on both sides (about 1 minute on each side). Do not burn garlic. Remove chicken from pan.

Deglaze pan with lemon juice and white wine. Add capers and butter. Reduce for 1 minute. Taste and adjust seasonings. Return chicken to pan, coat each side with sauce, and place on serving plate with sauce.

Cook's Tip: *The secret to tender, succulent piccata is to pound the meat as thin as possible with a meat mallet or similar tool. To save time, you can also ask the butcher to do this step for you.*

4 boneless, skinless chicken breast halves, pounded thin, seasoned with salt and pepper
Flour for dusting
1 tablespoon olive oil
1 teaspoon chopped garlic
2 teaspoons chopped onion
1 tablespoon fresh lemon juice
$1/4$ cup white wine
1 teaspoon capers, drained
6 tablespoons butter (3 ounces or $3/4$ cup)

Lemon Chicken with Penne

Bravo! Ristorante is a fun restaurant in which the waiters and waitresses sing for *your* supper during the dinner hour. It's also a popular place for requests such as this.

SERVES 4

Heat oil in pan, add garlic and shallot and sauté for 2 to 3 minutes. Deglaze pan with white wine and reduce.

Add chicken strips. Sauté for 3 to 4 minutes.

Add heavy cream and Gorgonzola and reduce liquid by half. Next, add asparagus, diced tomatoes, Parmesan, fresh herbs, and lemon juice and heat.

Add penne to pan and let it cook just until heated through. Add salt and pepper to taste. Garnish with basil and serve.

3 tablespoons olive oil
1 clove garlic, minced
1 small shallot, chopped
$1/2$ cup white wine
1 pound skinless, boneless chicken breasts, cut into strips
2 cups heavy cream
$1/2$ cup crumbled Gorgonzola
1 cup 2-inch asparagus pieces
1 cup fresh diced tomatoes
2 tablespoons grated Parmesan
Pinch of mixed fresh or dried herbs (thyme, rosemary, parsley, oregano, and chives)
2 tablespoons fresh lemon juice
Salt and pepper to taste
1 pound penne, cooked and drained
Fresh basil for garnish

· ·

Chicken Normandy

This is my kind of recipe—easy enough to whip up for the family for a weeknight dinner. Because of its volatility, be careful when adding the brandy—or any alcohol—to deglaze the pan. Deglazing the pan loosens up all those delicious browned bits on the bottom of the pan to give an added dimension to the sauce.

SERVES 4

Dredge the chicken breasts in flour. Sauté chicken in the olive or vegetable oil until cooked through (about 1 to 2 minutes each side). Remove the chicken from the pan. Over high heat, add brandy (again, be careful) to deglaze the pan, scraping up the browned bits from the bottom, and boiling to cook off the alcohol. Pour in the cream and apple juice and reduce heat; cook until sauce is creamy. Return chicken to pan with sauce; heat and serve, garnishing with apple slices.

4 to 6 boneless skinless chicken
   breast halves, pounded thin
Flour
2 tablespoons olive or vegetable oil
2 tablespoons brandy
1 cup whipping cream
1/4 cup apple juice
Apple slices for garnish

· ·

Almond-Encrusted Chicken with Cranberry and Cream Sauce

This is an interesting variation on breaded chicken with an easy-to-make cream sauce from Jay Witlen, the owner of Jay's.

SERVES 4

Preheat oven to 350 degrees.

Mix together panko, flour, and almonds, and add salt and pepper. Coat chicken breasts in beaten egg. Then dip in panko and almond mixture to form a crust. Heat oil in sauté pan. Brown chicken on both sides, then transfer to a baking dish. Cook in oven for 15 minutes or until cooked through.

To serve, pour Cranberry and Cream Sauce over chicken or spoon sauce onto plate and serve chicken atop sauce.

1 cup panko
1/4 cup all-purpose flour
1/2 cup sliced almonds
1 teaspoon each salt and pepper
4 boneless chicken breast halves,
   skin removed
1 egg, beaten
4 tablespoons oil
Cranberry and Cream Sauce
   (see recipe that follows)

Cook's Tip: *Panko, which are Japanese-style bread crumbs, can be found with other commercial bread crumbs or in the Asian food section of the grocery. It's interesting to note that when the experts at* Cook's Illustrated *tested commercial bread crumbs, panko came in first because of its "crisp" texture and "toasty," "wheaty" flavor.*

Cranberry and Cream Sauce

MAKES 2¹/₂ CUPS

Bring stock and juice to a boil. Off the heat, add amaretto and return to heat. Let alcohol cook out (about 1 minute); add heavy cream. Let reduce for 5 to 10 minutes. Add salt and pepper to taste and thicken to desired consistency with roux. Add dried cranberries.

1 cup chicken stock
1 cup cranberry juice
2 tablespoons amaretto
1 cup heavy cream
Salt and pepper to taste
¹/₄ cup roux or more, as required (equal parts flour and butter cooked together)
¹/₄ cup dried cranberries

Sesame Chicken

This was our very first request and restaurateur Johnny Hsu was kind enough to share the recipe, even though it's one of his signature dishes. Although the crunchy chicken of the original is difficult to attain in a home kitchen, this recipe will help you come close enough— and the sauce is right on the money. You'll get best results stir-frying the chicken in a wok.

SERVES 3 TO 4

In a small bowl, mix first 8 ingredients until well blended.

Cut chicken breasts into 1/2-inch strips. Place in bowl with water and salt and let soak for 15 minutes. Do not drain. Add cornstarch and mix well, coating chicken. Add 1 tablespoon oil to chicken and mix to smooth and separate chicken strips.

Heat wok on medium, pour in oil for deep-frying. Heat oil to 325 degrees. Place coated chicken strips in piece by piece and fry until crispy and cooked through (about 2 to 3 minutes). Remove chicken and place on wire racks to drain excess oil.

Heat wok again with an additional 1 teaspoon salad oil. Add ginger, garlic, and chili oil, stir-

8 tablespoons chicken broth
1 tablespoon dark soy sauce
2 tablespoons soy sauce
4 tablespoons sugar
4 tablespoons white vinegar
1 teaspoon cornstarch
1 teaspoon sake
1/2 teaspoon oyster sauce
1 pound skinless and boneless
   chicken breasts
6 tablespoons water
Pinch salt
5 tablespoons cornstarch
1 tablespoon vegetable oil
1/2 teaspoon peeled and minced gingerroot
1/2 teaspoon chopped garlic
1/2 to 1 teaspoon chili oil
1/2 teaspoon toasted sesame seeds
Vegetable oil for deep frying
Iceberg lettuce

frying until fragrant. Add sauce mix; stir until thickened. Add fried chicken strips and mix well to coat all chicken strips with sauce. Sprinkle on toasted sesame seeds before serving on a bed of lettuce.

Chicken and Penne with Roasted Chile Sauce

Palette's is one of the restaurants owned by Chef Kevin Taylor. This sauce gets its flavor from chicken broth, chiles, and roasted vegetables.

SERVES 8

To roast garlic: Pull off the papery outside and place the whole head in a pan with a little water on the bottom. Drizzle with olive oil. Cook at 400 degrees for 40 to 45 minutes. Squeeze garlic from cloves.

To roast tomatoes and peppers: Place tomatoes cut side down on a pan. Place red bell peppers and jalapeño pepper on same baking pan. Brush all with olive oil. Place under broiler for 5 minutes; turn tomatoes and peppers and broil 5 additional minutes. Remove pan from oven and carefully remove tomatoes. (If jalapeño is blackened, also remove it from pan.) Place pan back under broiler. Continue to char the peppers, turning to blacken all sides. When peppers are thoroughly charred, remove from oven and place jalapeño and bell peppers in a plastic bag. Allow to cool to loosen the skins. Rub off skins.

1 large head of garlic
4 Roma tomatoes, halved
2 red bell peppers, halved and seeded
1 jalapeño pepper, halved and seeded
1 tablespoon olive oil, plus oil for
   brushing tomatoes and peppers
1 shallot, minced
1 sprig fresh rosemary
1 sprig fresh thyme
1 pinch crushed dried red pepper flakes,
   or more to taste
2 cups chicken stock
4 grilled boneless, skinless chicken
   breast halves, sliced
3/4 pound dried penne, cooked and drained
Corn kernels cut from 2 ears of corn
Chopped scallions for garnish
Sour cream for garnish

Sauté the shallot, the garlic puree, and the herbs in the oil until the shallot is translucent. Add peppers, tomatoes, red pepper flakes, and chicken stock and bring to a boil. Simmer, covered, for 20 minutes.

(continued on next page)

Place tomato and pepper mixture in a food processor or blender and puree until smooth. Season to taste with salt and pepper. Strain through a sieve. Toss sliced grilled chicken, corn, and penne with sauce. Garnish with scallions and sour cream and serve.

Cook's Tip: I was short of time one day, so I tried the recipe without roasting the garlic (which tacks on an extra hour). I cut up garlic and sautéed it. I thought the sauce was still flavorful and delicious. I also tried the recipe with dried rosemary and thyme, which I had on hand, and frozen corn. Use a big pinch of the dried herbs (but remember that you won't need as much of the dried herb as you do the fresh) and heat the frozen corn briefly before adding to the sauce at the end.

Chicken with Anasazi Mix and Chipotle Cream Sauce

Owner and Executive Chef Bob Starekow has been a restaurant owner since 1975. Starekow also credits Chef Bruce Ganoung and Chef Barb Sneider for this interesting recipe.

SERVES 4

To make Anasazi mix: Combine first 8 ingredients. Add crab meat; mix together.

Next, prepare Chipotle Cream Sauce.

Preheat oven to 400 degrees.

While sauce is cooking, thoroughly coat chicken breasts in the cornmeal-flour mixture. Sauté in butter or olive oil until each side is a light golden brown. Prepare a glass baking dish with cooking spray and place sautéed breasts in dish.

Top each breast with a heaping tablespoon of the crab mixture; then place a fresh tomato slice on top of that.

Bake chicken for about 10 minutes until cooked through. Serve with the chipotle sauce and a few minced scallions sprinkled on top.

4 ounces cream cheese, softened
1/2 cup shredded pepperjack cheese
1/2 teaspoon ground cumin
1/2 teaspoon ground coriander
1/2 teaspoon crushed red pepper flakes
1/2 teaspoon chili powder
1 tablespoon grated yellow onion
1 egg, beaten
6 to 8 ounces shredded crab meat
Chipotle Cream Sauce
    (see recipe that follows)
4 boneless, skinless chicken breast halves
1/3 cup each of cornmeal and flour on a
    plate, seasoned with salt and pepper
Butter or olive oil for sautéing
1 large ripe tomato, cut into slices
Scallions, minced, for garnish

Note: You will have sauce and Anasazi mix left over. Both are great over omelets or grilled steak.

(continued on next page)

Chipotle Cream Sauce

MAKES 4^1/$_2$ CUPS

Make a roux of equal parts flour and melted butter, cooked until nut-brown.

Sauté the onion in a little butter or olive oil in a medium saucepan until wilted; add the cream, oyster sauce, and wine. Bring to a soft boil and add the chipotles and roux.

Pour into blender for a minute and blend, then return to saucepan and continue to cook at low boil for 30 minutes—long enough to thicken sauce and coat the spoon.

1 tablespoon roux (equal parts
    flour and butter cooked together)
^{1}/$_2$ yellow onion, grated
Butter or olive oil for sautéing
1 quart heavy cream
1 tablespoon oyster sauce
    (available in Asian food section)
1 cup white wine
3 chipotle peppers, minced (may use
    dried and rehydrated; see directions
    on package), or canned in adobo sauce
    and rinsed; be sure to stem and seed
    the peppers
1 scallion, minced, for garnish

Anasazi Chicken Enchiladas

Chef Scotty Krick reduced the recipe to serve four at home—no small task when you're cooking in large quantities for a restaurant. These enchiladas are named for the Anasazi ruins at nearby Mesa Verde National Park. The dish is one of the brewpub's best sellers, along with its award-winning Steam Engine Lager.

SERVES 4

Place diced chicken breast in a half-gallon pot. Add tomato, garlic, onion, chiles, cumin, and the bouillon, stirring constantly on low heat until chicken is cooked, about 20 minutes.

Add cream cheese, sour cream, and pepperjack cheese, stirring constantly until the pepperjack has melted.

Roll 6 tablespoons ($^5/_8$ cup) of the filling into each of 8 corn tortillas and place in a 9 × 13-inch casserole dish; smother them with the enchilada sauce (you may have some left over) and top with shredded Monterey Jack cheese.

$1^1/4$ pounds diced chicken breasts
$^1/2$ cup diced tomato
1 teaspoon diced garlic
$^1/2$ cup yellow onion, diced
4 ounces diced green chiles
Pinch ground cumin
1 teaspoon chicken bouillon
2 tablespoons cream cheese
$^1/4$ cup sour cream
$^1/4$ cup shredded pepperjack cheese
8 8-inch corn tortillas
$2^1/2$ cups Rosarita enchilada sauce
   or similar brand
$1^1/2$ cups shredded Monterey Jack cheese
$^1/2$ cup plain yogurt for garnish

Bake at 350 degrees for about 10 to 15 minutes or until cheese melts and casserole is hot. Remove from the oven and drizzle with yogurt. Serve with fresh chopped tomatoes, sour cream, guacamole, rice, and beans.

Fish & Seafood

Ligurian Stewed Scallops

After incredible success, Chef/owner Sean Kelly closed Aubergine and took a break. He re-opened with a new name, a new concept, and a new location. At Clair de Lune, he presides over a restaurant that has just eight tables and serves dinner only, where he can dish up his superb cuisine in a more personal way. For this recipe, "stewed" is a style of cooking seafood from a region in Italy: It combines fish stock and basil puree for delicious results.

SERVES 4

Choose a metal-handled pan large enough to easily hold scallops in one layer and with sides high enough to hold all the ingredients and place over high heat. Add 1 tablespoon oil and heat until very hot. Add scallops and sear until flesh begins to get a caramel color; turn and repeat to finish on other side (this will only take about 1 minute per side). When seared on both sides, transfer scallops to a plate and cover loosely with aluminum foil.

$1^{1}/_{2}$ pounds sea or bay scallops
2 tablespoons olive oil
2 teaspoons chopped garlic
2 cups cooked potatoes,
    peeled and diced large
$^{1}/_{4}$ to $^{1}/_{2}$ teaspoon crushed red pepper
    or more to taste
$^{1}/_{2}$ pound haricots verts (French string beans,
    available in the specialty produce aisle of
    the grocery), trimmed and blanched
1 to $1^{1}/_{2}$ cups Mediterranean or Moroccan
    black olives, oil-cured, pitted
2 cups fish fumet (fish stock), strained,
    or clam juice
6 tablespoons basil puree (puree $^{1}/_{4}$ cup
    basil leaves with 6 tablespoons olive oil)
Sea salt to taste
Fresh ground pepper to taste

Drain all pan juices and discard. Place pan back on burner and add 1 tablespoon remaining olive oil.

(continued on next page)

Over medium heat, add garlic and cooked potatoes and heat just until potatoes are warmed through. Add crushed red pepper, haricots verts, and olives and heat to warm everything through. Return scallops to pan, add fish stock, and bring to a simmer for 3 to 4 minutes; scallops will be opaque. Remove vegetables with slotted spoon and arrange on warmed serving platter; then remove scallops and place on top of vegetables. Off the heat, add basil puree to fish stock in pan and stir to combine; pour over scallops and veggies. Serve.

Cook's Tips: The difference between sea scallops and bay scallops is in size. Sea scallops are much larger, and bay scallops are small. Also, the bay scallops are slightly sweeter in taste. Sear the scallops first but don't overcook them, because they will cook again in the sauce. Cook the potatoes first until tender but not mushy.

To make your own fish stock, just ask your local seafood market for several pounds of fish trimmings, then add the usual suspects—carrots, onion, celery, parsley, wine and/or water, bay leaves, and peppercorns—and simmer for an hour. Strain and use.

Seared Scallops with Roasted Red and Yellow Pepper Sauces

The recipe uses two sauces—one using red peppers and one using yellow peppers. To make both sauces, you will have to make the sauce base twice: once with red peppers, once with yellow peppers. Since the scallops cook very quickly, be sure to make the sauces first, keeping them warm until serving.

SERVES 8

Season scallops with salt and pepper and sear in an extremely hot sauté pan with a little olive oil, cooking mostly on the first side of the scallop until nice and caramelized.

When turning the scallops over in the pan, add some frisee, white wine, and a dash of quality aged balsamic, salt, pepper, crushed red pepper, and a pinch of sugar. Wilt greens briefly (just a second). When scallops are cooked—3 to 4 minutes, until opaque—set aside.

For presentation, place the two separate pepper sauces side by side in the middle of a plate and arrange scallops on either side of the ribbon of sauces. Serve with mashed potatoes if desired.

40 sea scallops
(5 large sea scallops per serving)
Salt and pepper to taste
1 to 2 tablespoons olive oil
Frisee or other sturdy, curly greens
2 tablespoons white wine
Dash of balsamic vinegar
Crushed red pepper to taste
Pinch of sugar
Mashed potatoes (optional)

Cook's Tip: To roast peppers, char over a grill or under a broiler on all sides. Place in plastic bag to sweat. When cool enough to handle, peel off outer skins and seed.

(continued on next page)

Roasted Red and Yellow Pepper Sauces

MAKES ENOUGH FOR 8 TO 10 SERVINGS

In a heavy-bottomed saucepan (large enough to hold the quart of chicken stock), cook the garlic and peppers in oil, covered, until slightly softened.

Deglaze the pan with the wine and tequila and cook until the pan is almost dry. Add the honey and stock and cook until reduced by a quarter; add the cream and cook until sauce thickens (do not boil).

Adjust seasonings with salt, pepper, and crushed red pepper to taste.

Remove from heat. Add cilantro and puree until smooth. Strain through a fine mesh strainer.

1 quart chicken stock
4 cloves garlic, minced
1 pound yellow or red peppers,
   roasted, peeled, and seeded
1 to 2 tablespoons olive oil
$^1/_4$ cup white wine
$^1/_4$ cup tequila
$^1/_4$ cup honey
1 cup heavy cream
Salt, pepper, and crushed
   red pepper to taste
Pinch fresh cilantro leaves

Brian's Shrimp

This simple recipe from Chef Brian Durbin of the popular Carmine's on Penn is another good choice when company's coming and you need something quick, but elegant, for dinner. Always have a bag of frozen peeled and deveined shrimp on hand, and you're ready anytime. A nice touch is to finish the dish with a sprinkle of one of the specialty sea salts, available at supermarkets and at gourmet kitchenware stores.

SERVES 4

Peel and devein shrimp and set aside.

Wash and prepare spinach leaves; be sure to dry well, then remove stems. Set spinach and basil aside. Toast the pine nuts in a 325-degree oven until golden. Watch carefully; the nuts are very delicate and take only a few moments to toast.

Cook pasta in boiling, salted water until it's three-quarters of the way cooked (use package instructions to determine cooking time). Meanwhile, in a pot large enough to hold all the ingredients, including pasta, heat both oils

1 pound raw jumbo shrimp
10 ounces fresh spinach
1/4 cup julienned fresh basil
1/3 cup pine nuts
3/4 pound linguine
1/4 cup virgin olive oil
1/4 cup canola oil
2 large cloves garlic, sliced
1/2 teaspoon salt
1/2 teaspoon pepper
3/4 cup dry white wine
3/4 cup low-sodium chicken broth
Sea salt (optional)

over medium heat. Add the sliced garlic. When the garlic chips are golden brown, add all the spinach; next, sprinkle the pine nuts over the spinach.

When spinach begins to wilt, stir it and then place the shrimp on top of the leaves. Salt and pepper the mixture.

(continued on next page)

Next, sprinkle the basil over the shrimp. Add the white wine and chicken broth and allow the shrimp to cook just until they turn pink. Add the pasta and toss; allow pasta to finish cooking in the sauce until all the sauce is absorbed. Salt and pepper generously or sprinkle with sea salt. Serve immediately.

Cook's Tip: The coarser grain of sea salt adds a nice touch to enhance a dish, adding a flavor punch (its taste is more truly a taste of the sea, without the metallic flavor of mined salt). A little goes a long way, so use with a light hand. I used Grey Sea Salt for this dish.

Tomato Shrimp

Red Coral, a family-friendly Chinese restaurant, makes this dish with beef or with shrimp. I like it both ways—but if I had to choose, it would be this version.

SERVES 4

Add vegetable oil to heated wok. Add ginger, garlic, and green onion, green pepper, and onion and sauté lightly until vegetables begin to soften.

Stir in ketchup and sugar. Next, pour in chicken broth. Mix and stir the ingredients quickly over high heat until sugar is dissolved. Add the peas (or pea-carrot mixture), tomato, and shrimp to sauce and sauté until shrimp are just cooked (they should be pink).

Season with white or black pepper and 3 to 4 dashes of sesame oil. Serve immediately over cooked rice.

1 tablespoon vegetable oil
1 teaspoon peeled and minced gingerroot
1 teaspoon minced garlic
1 green onion, diced
1 small green pepper, cut into cubes
1 small yellow onion, cut into cubes
1/2 cup ketchup
A scant 1/3 cup sugar (you can start with even less and add more, if sauce isn't sweet enough for your taste)
1/4 cup chicken broth
1/2 cup peas or mixture of peas and diced carrot
1 large tomato, cut into cubes
15 to 20 medium-sized raw shrimp, peeled and deveined
White or black pepper to taste
Sesame oil to taste
Cooked rice for 4

Shrimp Parisienne

This dish from Chef Michael Bortz would make a good first or main course at a company dinner.

SERVES 4

Mix all ingredients in a glass bowl, except shrimp and Lemon Butter Sauce. Add shrimp and mix well. Cover tightly and allow shrimp to marinate overnight in refrigerator.

Remove shrimp from marinade; discard marinade. Grill or broil until shrimp turn pink, about $1^1/2$ minutes per side. Prepare sauce. Ladle sauce onto plate, placing shrimp on top of sauce. Serve immediately.

> 2 tablespoons white wine
> 1 tablespoon olive oil
> 2 tablespoons ketchup
> $1/4$ teaspoon red chili flakes
> $1^1/2$ teaspoons granulated garlic
> $1^1/2$ teaspoons basil
> $1^1/2$ teaspoons tarragon
> 1 pound raw shrimp, peeled and deveined
> Lemon Butter Sauce
>   (see recipe that follows)

Lemon Butter Sauce

MAKES $1^1/2$ CUPS

In a saucepan, combine cream and lemon juice. Reduce to about $1/4$ cup liquid over low heat; mixture will be very thick. Remove from heat. Add butter. Keep temperature constant— sauce will separate if too hot or cold. Season with salt and pepper.

> $1/2$ cup plus 2 tablespoons heavy cream
> Juice from 1 lemon
> 2 sticks butter ($1/2$ pound or 1 cup),
>   softened

Grilled Ahi Tuna with Kalamata Olive Vinaigrette

Chef Jennifer Jasinski made a name for herself during her years at Panzano, whether she was dishing up dinner or dessert. You'll want top-quality sashimi-grade Ahi tuna for this dish.

SERVES 2

Roast or broil red and yellow peppers until blackened; place in closed plastic bag to sweat for about 15 minutes; peel off skin. Seed and julienne.

Heat sauté pan until hot, add olive oil, garlic, bell peppers, and Swiss chard and cook until chard is wilted. Pile mixture on a warmed serving plate.

Broil or grill tuna about 2 minutes per side. Slice grilled tuna, cutting diagonally, and place fanned-out slices on top of chard and peppers mixture. Drizzle with vinaigrette.

2 7-ounce steaks of sashimi-grade
   Ahi tuna, seasoned with
   kosher salt and ground pepper
1 red bell pepper
1 yellow bell pepper
2 tablespoons olive oil
1 teaspoon chopped garlic
1 large bunch Swiss chard,
   stems removed and washed
Kalamata Olive Vinaigrette
   (see recipe that follows)

Kalamata Olive Vinaigrette

MAKES 2 CUPS

Mix all ingredients, whisking in olive oil until blended.

$1/2$ cup pitted, roughly chopped kalamata
   olives
$1/2$ teaspoon chopped garlic
$1/2$ teaspoon chopped chives
$1/2$ cup white balsamic vinegar
Salt and pepper to taste
$1^1/2$ cups extra-virgin olive oil

Stir-Fry Fish with Cashews

New Orient restaurant is a gem of a Vietnamese place. Owner Sue Smith provided this recipe.

SERVES 4 TO 6

Cook sugar and water in a small saucepan over high heat. Bring to a boil and start to stir; stir constantly until the sugar syrup turns brown and starts to thicken. Watch carefully or it will burn. Remove from heat; add soy sauce and pinch of salt and stir. Set aside.

Working quickly, heat oil in a wok or frying pan over high heat. Add garlic, fish, lemongrass, fish sauce, and onion. Stir-fry the fish for about 3 minutes (if using shrimp, stir-fry until shrimp turn pink). Add the sugar-soy syrup, the broccoli and snow peas, cashews, and chili flakes. Remove from the heat immediately and sprinkle fish with sesame seeds. Serve over rice.

Cook's Tips: Nuoc mam is a fish sauce used in Vietnamese cooking (the Thai fish sauce is called nam pla). It smells unpleasant in the bottle, but as it cooks in a sauce, it adds good flavor to the dish. *Because of its salty undertones, nuoc mam is often used in place of soy sauce in Vietnamese cooking.*

^{1}/2 cup sugar
^{1}/2 cup water
3 tablespoons soy sauce
Pinch salt
2 tablespoons vegetable oil
1 clove garlic, minced
10 to 12 ounces fish fillets (mahimahi or sea bass), sliced ^{1}/2-inch thick, or 1 pound raw shrimp, peeled and deveined
1 stalk lemongrass, finely minced
2 teaspoons fish sauce (nuoc mam), available in the Asian section of groceries
1 onion, sliced
1 cup steamed broccoli florets
1 cup steamed snow peas
^{1}/2 cup cashews
Red chili flakes
Sesame seeds for garnish
Cooked rice

Lemongrass is available fresh in the produce aisle or dried in the spice aisle at the grocery. Mince it very finely or it will ruin the dish, because it will be stringy and inedible.

Note that the syrup starts off the way you would make caramel, which means that it's easy to burn if you let it cook even 30 seconds too long. Take it off the stove sooner rather than later, because it will continue to cook. If it thickens up too much as it cools while you prepare the rest of the recipe, you can place the pan of syrup in hot water and stir it until it melts to sauce consistency.

Sautéed Grouper with Sweet Pea Basil Sauce and Asparagus

This was an offering on a special Garden Party menu at the acclaimed restaurant in the Brown Palace Hotel. If you have trouble finding grouper, substitute another fish. The sauce is very rich.

SERVES 4

Blend half the peas in a blender with chicken stock to obtain a smooth puree. Sauté the fish fillets in 2 to 3 tablespoons of butter until done (8 to 10 minutes), remove, and set aside. Cover lightly with foil. In the same pan, sauté the shallots in half of the truffle oil very briefly. Add the pea puree and basil, and bring to a gentle simmer. Whisk in the butter, and season with salt and pepper. Add the remaining peas.

Preheat oven to 400 degrees.

Lay 8 spears of blanched asparagus, grouped together to resemble a raft, on each ovenproof plate. Brush the spears with truffle oil and warm them briefly in the oven. Remove from oven and lay the fish fillets on top of the asparagus "raft," covering the cut ends of the stalks. Ladle the sauce over the asparagus and around the plate. Serve immediately.

$1^{1}/_{2}$ pounds fresh shelled peas,
   or frozen baby peas, thawed
1 cup chicken stock
   (if freshly made, be sure it has cooled)
4 7- to 8-ounce grouper fillets
   (if you can't find grouper,
   red snapper is a good substitute)
$^{1}/_{2}$ stick unsalted butter, plus 2 to 3
   tablespoons for sautéing fish
$^{1}/_{4}$ cup minced shallots
$^{1}/_{4}$ cup truffle oil
2 tablespoons julienned basil
32 asparagus spears, blanched

Cook's Tip: Truffle oil, which is olive oil infused with truffles, has become a popular ingredient in the last few years. You'll find it at specialty groceries or kitchen stores.

∙ ∙

Potato-Crusted Halibut with Crisp Potato Cake, Creamed Spinach, and Red Wine Sauce

Chef/Restaurateur Kevin Taylor has received numerous accolades for his cooking. This dish wowed the Swiss dignitaries at a luncheon. It's a delicious, fairly spectacular recipe and, although it seems like it has a lot of steps, it's not that difficult when broken down into its parts. The flavor and texture combination is incredible. If you have company you want to impress, this is a good choice.

SERVES 4

3 cups red wine (nearly a whole bottle)
12 new potatoes
1 1/2 pounds halibut fillet, cut into 4 pieces
10 ounces fresh baby spinach,
   washed and patted dry
1/2 cup heavy cream
2 sticks unsalted butter (8 ounces or 1 cup)
Fresh or dried herbs for garnish

To make red wine sauce: Bring red wine to a boil; simmer gently until reduced to 1 cup (takes about an hour). Finish with 2 tablespoons butter; cover and turn off heat.

To make the crisp potato cake: Slice potatoes into very thin rounds. Melt 1 stick of butter and toss sliced potatoes in it, coating well.

Reserve 24 potato slices to cook with the fish. Place remaining slices in a small stovetop-safe and ovenproof pan, spiraling them until 3 layers cover the pan bottom. Put pan on burner on medium heat until bottom of potatoes brown well. Set aside.

To prepare the halibut: Place fillets skin-side-down. Arrange 6 potato rounds in an overlapping pattern on top of each fillet.

Heat a sauté pan over medium-high heat with 3 tablespoons clarified butter (melted, with milk fats skimmed off). Sear fillets potato-side-down until brown; turn fillets over and sear skin side. Remove pan from heat and place browned fillets, potato-side-up, into glass baking dish coated in cooking spray.

(continued on next page)

∙ ∙

Preheat oven to 400 degrees.

Cook potato cakes in oven until crisp on top, about 15 to 20 minutes; for last 5 minutes, put fillets in oven to finish cooking (make sure fish is cooked through).

To make the creamed spinach: Sauté spinach over medium-high heat in 3 tablespoons butter. When spinach is very wilted, add cream—turn off heat when bubbly, cover, but leave pan on the cooling burner.

To serve: Place a serving of potato cake on plate, top with creamed spinach, then the fillet. Spoon the red wine sauce around the potato cake and garnish with fresh or dried herbs.

Cook's Tips: Slice the potatoes as thinly as possible, using a food processor or a mandoline, if possible. (A mandoline is a special slicing tool—not a musical instrument—that will help you slice vegetables as thinly and artfully as you like.)

If you prefer not to make your own clarified butter, you can buy it at food specialty stores.

Barbecue Salmon with Blue Corn Cakes and Cilantro Crema

Another of Chef Kevin Taylor's dishes from one of his restaurants, this recipe requires a lot of steps because it has three major elements—corn cakes, salmon, and a sauce to drizzle on top. Don't be intimidated: Just take it one step at a time, and impress your guests with a special Southwest-inspired entree.

SERVES 6

Brush salmon with barbecue sauce and grill or broil until done (check at 5 minutes). Divide salmon into 6 portions and place on top of hot

2^1/$_2$ pounds salmon fillets
1 cup commercial barbecue sauce
   (your choice)
6 Blue Corn Cakes (see recipe that follows)
^{1}/$_2$ cup Cilantro Crema
   (see recipe that follows)
6 sprigs fresh cilantro

corn cakes; drizzle Cilantro Crema over the salmon. Garnish with a drizzle of warm barbecue sauce and a sprig of fresh cilantro.

Blue Corn Cakes

MAKES 6 CAKES

Mix all ingredients in large mixing bowl. Ladle about ^{1}/$_2$ cup of batter per pancake (you should have 6 total) onto a hot griddle or nonstick sauté pan. (Pancakes can be made smaller; allow 2 per person.) Cook over low heat until golden brown on each side, about 3 minutes per side. Place corn cakes on an ovenproof plate, cover loosely with foil, and place in oven at lowest heat to keep warm while cooking the salmon.

Fresh corn kernels cut from 2 ears corn
^{1}/$_2$ bunch green onions, chopped
^{1}/$_2$ red pepper, seeded and diced
4 serrano chiles, finely diced
1 cup flour
1 cup blue cornmeal
^{3}/$_4$ teaspoon baking powder
^{3}/$_4$ teaspoon ground cumin
2 cups half-and-half
^{1}/$_2$ stick melted butter (2 ounces or ^{1}/$_4$ cup)
2 egg whites, beaten until stiff
^{1}/$_2$ teaspoon salt
^{1}/$_4$ teaspoon pepper

(continued on next page)

Cilantro Crema

MAKES 1 CUP

Stir first 3 ingredients together and season to taste with salt and pepper.

1 cup sour cream
1 bunch cilantro, chopped
1 teaspoon fresh lime juice
Salt and pepper to taste

Scandinavian Salmon

Everyone should have a good cucumber-dill sauce in his or her repertoire to serve with salmon. The recipe for the sauce in this dish is delicious and fits the bill. You can dress up the plate with mashed or roasted potatoes and steamed fresh vegetables.

SERVES 8

Grill salmon to desired degree of doneness. The best technique is to lightly oil your grill beforehand (rub cooking grate with paper towels dipped in oil). Once coals are ready, place the salmon fillets skin side down and grill until the skins shrink and turn black (about 2 to 3 minutes). Gently turn over the fillets and

2^1/$_2$ pounds center-cut salmon fillets, seasoned with salt and pepper
Cucumber-Dill Sauce
(see recipe that follows)

grill for about another 3 to 4 minutes. To serve, place salmon on warmed platter and top with Cucumber-Dill Sauce, or serve sauce alongside.

Cook's Tip: To roast potatoes, cut small skin-on red potatoes into quarters. Place in roasting pan and lightly pour olive oil over the potatoes to moisten them. Sprinkle with salt and cook at 400 degrees until brown and crispy, about 1 hour.

Cucumber-Dill Sauce

MAKES 2^3/$_4$ CUPS

Combine all ingredients and mix well. Taste to adjust for seasonings.

2 cups yogurt
^{1}/4 to ^{1}/2 cup honey to taste
^{1}/2 cup Dijon mustard
1 teaspoon cracked pepper
2 teaspoons dried dill
2 tablespoons chopped fresh dill
1 cup cucumber, peeled, seeded, and chopped

McCormick's Fish House and Bar

Salmon with Beurre Rouge Sauce

Longtime McCormick's chef Steven Vice cooks the salmon on a cedar plank, which has become such a popular technique that the planks are sold in any gourmet kitchenware store. You may, however, prepare the salmon with any method you like.

SERVES 4

Combine red wine, red wine vinegar, peppercorns, rosemary, and shallot in a non-aluminum saucepan. Over medium heat, reduce mixture to 1 to 2 tablespoons, with the consistency of syrup. Add cream and reduce again to 3 to 4 tablespoons and very syrupy. Remove pan from heat. (It will take 45 minutes to do both reductions.) The salmon will take about 10 minutes to cook, depending on the method you choose, so be sure to time this process to begin toward the end of the reduction of the sauce.

Add butter to sauce, once piece at a time, stirring constantly and allowing each addition to melt in before adding more. (If mixture cools too much, butter will not melt completely and you'll have to reheat slightly.) Strain and serve sauce on the side with salmon.

3/4 cup red wine
1/4 cup plus 2 tablespoons red wine vinegar
3 whole peppercorns
1 sprig fresh rosemary
1 shallot, cut into quarters
1 cup heavy cream
1 1/2 pounds salmon fillets
2 sticks cold, unsalted butter, cut into pieces

Note: This sauce can be flavored with orange or lemon, spices, herbs, berry or fruit concentrates. These may be added at the end or during reduction of the cream.

You may grill, poach, or broil salmon (use the 10 minutes-per-inch of thickness cooking rule). Serve with sauce.

Cook's Tip: *It will take you about 45 minutes to reduce the sauce, so plan ahead. This sauce is tricky to make because it will separate if it's overheated or cooked too long. Add the butter slowly at the end. If you see a film of oil begin to surface, take the sauce off the heat immediately and keep whisking. Make sauce just before serving, rather than trying to rewarm it.*

. . . .

Grilled Salmon with Molasses and Black Pepper Glaze

My note scribbled on the top of this recipe says: "Delicious, a real winner." Don't skip the Honey Vinaigrette (which can be made in advance).

SERVES 4 TO 6

Whisk together honey, vinegar, mustard, and molasses. Grill (or broil) salmon fillets skin side up for 3 to 4 minutes. Turn. Spoon or brush glaze on salmon. Sprinkle with cracked pepper. Continue cooking until done (3 to 4 minutes). Drizzle with Honey Vinaigrette and serve immediately.

Honey Vinaigrette

MAKES 1 1/2 CUPS

Mix all ingredients together except oil. Whip by hand or in a blender. Add oil slowly through the feed tube and continue to whip until emulsified.

---

1 1/2 to 2 pounds salmon fillets
1/8 cup honey
1/4 cup red wine vinegar
1/4 cup dry mustard
3/4 cup molasses
2 tablespoons cracked pepper
Honey Vinaigrette (see recipe that follows)

makes double the sauces needed

A scant 1/3 cup coarse-grain mustard
1/4 cup red wine vinegar
3 tablespoons honey
1 tablespoon molasses
1 tablespoon brown sugar
3/4 cup olive oil

. . . .

Baked Alaskan Salmon with Roasted Red Peppers and Capers

Restaurateur Mark Canino of Bambino's serves this recipe with grilled vegetables. This is a nice, easy recipe for entertaining. Although you can use canned roasted red peppers, I would recommend taking the extra step and roasting your own.

SERVES 4

Preheat oven to 400 degrees.

Season fillets with salt and pepper and place in a shallow baking dish.

Whisk together the garlic, olive oil, and wine and pour over the fillets. Sprinkle capers and peppers over top of fish and bake for 15 minutes or until fish is cooked through.

Salt and pepper to taste
1 1/2 pounds salmon fillets
4 cloves garlic, chopped
2 tablespoons olive oil
1 cup white wine
1 teaspoon capers, drained
1/2 cup roughly chopped
  roasted red bell peppers

Cook's Tip: In cooking fish, follow the so-called Canadian rule. Allow 10 minutes of cooking time for each inch of thickness. Another good test is to check the flesh at its thickest point. If it's opaque, the fish is cooked. To roast peppers, hold peppers over a flame with tongs, or place under the broiler on a cookie sheet. Turn frequently until skin is blackened. Remove from heat and place in a plastic bag to sweat for 15 minutes. Peel, stem, and seed.

Salmon with Balsamic Syrup and Orange Crème Fraîche

Owners Sue and Will McFarlane made buffalo a popular choice for diners, but their restaurant also had other delicious dishes. This salmon was the hit of a dinner party I had.

SERVES 4

Season fillets or steaks with salt and pepper. Poach, broil, or grill fish to your desired degree of doneness.

Place vinegar and sugar in a non-aluminum saucepan. Bring to a boil and keep mixture at a rolling boil, reducing heat if necessary. Reduce volume by half (10 to 15 minutes). Cool slightly and pour into a squeeze bottle for application.

Next, combine crème fraîche, juice, and zest and place in another squeeze bottle.

1 1/2 pounds salmon fillets or salmon steaks
Salt and pepper to taste
1 cup balsamic vinegar
3/4 cup brown sugar
1/2 cup crème fraîche
1/2 tablespoon orange juice concentrate
Juice from 1/2 of the orange (grate zest before juicing)
Zest from 1 orange, finely chopped

To serve, decorate individual serving plates with swirls of balsamic syrup and place fish on top. Squeeze crème fraîche decoratively on top of fish.

Cook's Tip: Crème fraîche, made from thickened cream, is available at many groceries and at most specialty food markets. If you can't find it, sour cream will do in a pinch.

Salmon with Shrimp Mashed Potatoes in Port Wine Sauce

Many of the ingredients in this recipe are for the Court Bouillon, the cooking liquid for the salmon, which can be prepared a day or two in advance. If you desire, you can skip making this and prepare the salmon any way you like. (It will still be a satisfying dish.) The sauce, however, doesn't hold well and must be made right before serving. Adding shrimp to mashed potatoes lends an interesting twist to an old favorite.

SERVES 4

Place salmon in simmering Court Bouillon and poach, uncovered, for 10 minutes per inch of thickness. Remove from bouillon and place on plate.

While salmon is cooking, prepare mashed potatoes and wine sauce.

Court Bouillon

MAKES 1^{1}/$_{2}$ QUARTS

Bring water to a boil. Add all remaining ingredients and simmer for about 30 minutes. If you are making ahead, cover and refrigerate at this point until ready for use.

> 1^{1}/$_{2}$ pounds salmon fillets
> Court Bouillon (see recipe that follows)
> Shrimp Mashed Potatoes (see recipe that follows)
> Port Wine Sauce (see recipe that follows)
> ^{1}/$_{2}$ cup chopped, diced tomato
> 8 ounces fresh spinach, washed, patted dry, and sliced into thin strips
> Chives for garnish

To serve, place a 1-inch bed of mashed potatoes on serving platter. Place fish over potatoes. Spoon tomatoes and spinach over fish; pour wine sauce around salmon and potatoes. Garnish with remaining whole shrimp and chives.

> 1 quart water
> 1 small bay leaf
> ^{1}/$_{4}$ cup chopped carrots
> ^{1}/$_{4}$ cup chopped celery
> 1 small onion stuck with two whole cloves
> ^{1}/$_{2}$ cup dry white wine
> 1 teaspoon salt
> 2 tablespoons chopped fresh parsley

Shrimp Mashed Potatoes

MAKES ENOUGH FOR 4 SERVINGS

Boil potatoes until tender, drain, and mash, adding milk and butter to desired taste. Cover and set aside. (The secret to good mashed potatoes is to warm the milk in the microwave before adding it to the hot potatoes.)

Sauté shrimp in butter until pink. Next, chop half of cooked shrimp and mix with chives into mashed potatoes. Save half the shrimp for garnish.

3 to 5 Yukon potatoes, peeled, chopped
4 to 6 tablespoons butter
1/4 cup warmed milk for
    making mashed potatoes
9 to 12 raw shrimp
1 tablespoon butter
1 to 2 tablespoons chopped
    fresh chives to taste

Port Wine Sauce

MAKES 1 1/8 CUPS

Pour port into a pan; cook over medium heat and reduce by half. Add remaining ingredients, whisking until butter is melted. Heat gently and briefly just to warm through. Strain sauce.

3/4 cup port wine
3/4 cup veal or beef stock
2 tablespoons chopped shallots
3 sprigs fresh thyme
1 small bay leaf
4 tablespoons butter

Chipotle-Glazed Salmon with Guacamole and Corn–Black Bean Salsa

The salmon with chipotle glaze is wonderful, even without the accompaniments. When I served this dish to company, some people opted to wrap the salmon in the tortilla with the guacamole and salsa; others chose to eat the tortilla alongside.

SERVES 4 TO 6

To prepare chipotle glaze: If using canned chipotles, pull out two chiles. No need to rinse. Set aside the remaining canned chipotles for the beans. Blend peppers, Worcestershire sauce, tomato paste, mustard, and vinegar until smooth. Slowly, while running blender, add apple juice.

Preheat oven to 400 degrees.

Place salmon fillets in glass baking dish, skin side down. Brush with chipotle glaze and bake until fish flakes easily. (Again, the 10-minute-per-inch of thickness rule will help you time this.)

To assemble: Spoon guacamole onto plate and top with corn-bean salsa mixture; place salmon on top. Serve with warm flour tortillas and rice.

2 chipotle peppers (you can use 2 peppers from canned whole chipotles in adobo sauce)
1 tablespoon Worcestershire sauce
2 tablespoons tomato paste
1 tablespoon Coleman's dry mustard
1 tablespoon red wine vinegar
1 cup apple juice
1 1/2 to 2 pounds salmon fillets
Guacamole (see recipe that follows)
Corn–Black Bean Salsa with Pico de Gallo (see recipe that follows)

Cook's Tip: The original recipe called for cooking dried black beans. After I forgot to soak the beans, I realized that they were never going to get soft, so I ran to the grocery and grabbed a couple cans of black beans. I followed the recipe, except that I drained the cans of beans and measured the equivalent of the dried beans. I cooked them just briefly with the chicken broth and the bay leaves and chipotles for flavor and went from there. The recipe has so much flavor that my shortcut didn't seem to make any real difference to the end result.

Guacamole

MAKES 1 CUP

Mash avocados by hand and mix in remaining ingredients or pulse in a food processor or blender to desired consistency.

Corn–Black Bean Salsa with Pico de Gallo

MAKES 2 1/2 CUPS

Simmer dried black beans, prepared according to package directions, in the chicken stock with the cumin, bay leaves, and chipotles, about 1 1/2 hours until tender. Strain beans and remove chipotles and bay leaves. While still warm, toss beans with oil, salt and pepper. Set aside to cool.

Cook corn kernels; drain. Spread a little oil on baking pan and sprinkle corn into pan. Salt and pepper, then broil for 7 to 10 minutes until lightly browned. Combine with beans.

Just before serving, combine remaining ingredients—which constitute a relish known as pico de gallo—with the corn-bean mixture.

---

2 ripe avocados
1 tomatillo, chopped
2 to 3 tablespoons fresh cilantro, chopped
1 jalapeño, seeded and chopped
Juice of 1/2 lime
Salt and pepper

---

1 cup dried black beans
1 quart chicken stock
1 teaspoon ground cumin
2 to 3 bay leaves
2 chipotle peppers (from canned)
2 tablespoons vegetable oil
Salt and pepper to taste
1 cup corn kernels, fresh or frozen
2 Roma tomatoes, seeded and diced
1 to 2 jalapeños, seeded and diced
Fresh chopped cilantro, to taste
1/2 small onion, diced small
Juice of 1 lime
Salt and pepper

Pasta, Vegetables, & Sides

(continued on next page)

Pasta, Vegetables, & Sides, *continued*

Chicken Penne with Gorgonzola, Grapes, and Walnuts

One of Bella Ristorante's most popular offerings, this dish combines lots of tastes and textures. Cook the pasta to al dente, which means firm (to the tooth).

SERVES 4

Heat sauté pan and add oil, onion, and garlic. Sauté until translucent. Add grilled chicken and heat through.

Deglaze with white wine, scraping up browned bits on the bottom of the pan. Add cream and Romano and reduce until slightly thickened (coats back of spoon).

Toss in cooked penne and heat. When pasta is heated through, add Gorgonzola. (Gorgonzola is a very strong blue cheese, so add sparingly at first and increase amount as desired.) Toss with grapes and walnuts. Season to taste with salt and pepper. Garnish with chopped parsley and Parmesan chips and serve.

$1^1/2$ teaspoons oil
2 tablespoons finely diced yellow onion
2 tablespoons chopped garlic
1 pound grilled chicken breasts,
    cut into strips
$1/4$ cup white wine
$1^1/4$ cups heavy cream
$1/4$ cup grated Romano
10 ounces dried penne, cooked al dente
$1/2$ cup plus 2 tablespoons
    crumbled Gorgonzola
1 handful red seedless grapes
2 tablespoons chopped walnuts
$1/4$ cup chopped parsley
Salt and pepper to taste
2 tablespoons Parmesan chips (optional)

Cook's Tip: To make Parmesan chips, which are also a nice garnish for a salad, slice Parmesan with a cheese slicer and bake at 350 degrees until pieces are golden brown.

Pasta with Chicken and Chipotle Salsa

Chef/owner Fred Bramhall of Bluepoint Bakery came up with this recipe for the original Chives restaurant.

SERVES 6 TO 8

Sear chicken in oil. Add julienned red and green peppers and sauté, adding a little oil if necessary and cooking until chicken is cooked through. Add cream and salsa and simmer until slightly thickened and reduced. Do not boil. Add Cheddar, if desired, and cooked pasta and heat for a minute more until cheese is melted and pasta is hot. Toss with chives before serving. Sprinkle with Romano, if desired.

Cook's Tips: *Canned chipotle chiles in adobo sauce are available at most grocery stores. A chipotle is a smoked jalapeño that imparts a rich, smoky flavor to any dish.*

Mostaccioli (which translates in Italian to "small mustaches") is similar to penne in its tube shape and sometimes has ridges, sometimes not.

$3/4$ pound skinless, boneless chicken, diced into cubes
1 tablespoon vegetable oil
1 red bell pepper, seeded and julienned
1 green bell pepper, seeded and julienned
2 cups heavy cream
1 cup Chipotle Salsa (see recipe that follows)
$1^1/3$ cups grated Cheddar (optional)
1 pound fresh linguine or mostaccioli, cooked and drained
1 tablespoon chopped fresh chives
Grated Romano (optional)

Chipotle Salsa

Place whole tomatoes on hot grill or under broiler and char on all sides until partially blackened. Do not peel. Place tomatoes, onions, garlic, and peppers with adobo sauce in food processor and puree until almost smooth, but still a little chunky. Pour mixture into saucepan; add oregano and vinegar and simmer for approximately 25 minutes until thickened. Add scallions and salt to taste.

4 tomatoes
1 onion, peeled and chopped
3 cloves garlic
3 chipotle peppers with adobo sauce
2 teaspoons oregano
2 tablespoons rice vinegar
3 scallions, green part only, minced
Salt to taste

Penne Alfredo with Grilled Chicken

Cheryl Brown, the chef/co-owner of Sage Southwestern Grill, has a delicious repertoire of dishes. This is certainly a uniquely Southwestern take on fettuccine Alfredo.

SERVES 4

Preheat oven to 350 degrees.

Dredge chicken breasts in mixture of olive oil and Cajun blackening seasoning and bake in oven for 20 minutes or until cooked through. Cut into strips.

Sauté garlic in a little olive oil until it starts to brown. Add pico de gallo, then the chicken strips and chili powder and cook until most of the liquid is gone.

Add cream and $1/2$ cup Parmesan. Bring to a simmer, add pasta and stir and cook until heated through and sauce has thickened. Serve in large bowls and top with grated Parmesan. Serve chopped green onion and chopped jalapeño on the side for those who like it really spicy.

4 boneless, skinless chicken breast halves
Olive oil for cooking
4 teaspoons chopped garlic
Cajun blackening seasoning
4 tablespoons pico de gallo
Ancho chili–garlic chili powder blend
   (can substitute any good chili powder
   with a little garlic powder added)
3 cups heavy whipping cream
$1/2$ cup grated Parmesan,
   plus additional for topping
Chopped green onions
4 teaspoons chopped jalapeños,
   seeds and ribs removed (optional)
4 servings cooked penne
   (about 10 ounces dried)

Cook's Tip: Cajun blackening seasoning is commonly available in the spice section of most grocery stores. Also, canned pico de gallo is available in the Mexican food section. However, you can make a fresh version of pico de gallo using the recipe on page 48 of this book.

Chicken Lo Mein

Restaurateur Johnny Hsu of the Imperial Chinese and Palace Chinese restaurants says that the secret to lo mein is to cook the noodles first, then panfry them. The distinctive flavor of this dish comes from the oyster sauce. This is an easy-to-prepare, kid-pleasing dinner.

SERVES ~~4~~ 6

Cut chicken into thin slices, then cut into 1/4-inch strips. Marinate chicken strips with a pinch of salt and 1 tablespoon salad oil. Set aside.

Bring water to boil on a stove. Cook fresh egg noodles according to instructions on the package. Separate strands with a fork so noodles don't clump. Put 1 tablespoon salad oil into noodles before the water is drained. The oil will help keep the noodles from becoming sticky. Drain. Set aside to cool.

Mix soy sauce, oyster sauce, sugar, and sesame oil in a small bowl.

Set wok over medium heat, put in 1 to 2 tablespoons salad oil and the minced ginger and

3 to 4 skinless, boneless chicken breast halves
Pinch of salt
3 to 4 tablespoons salad oil
Water for cooking noodles
8 ounces fresh egg noodles (found in the produce section of the grocery store)
2 tablespoons soy sauce
1 teaspoon oyster sauce *used 1 T.*
1/2 tablespoon sugar
1 teaspoon sesame oil *or sesame/chile*
1/2 teaspoon peeled and minced gingerroot
1/2 teaspoon minced garlic
1/2 cup shredded Napa cabbage
2 stalks celery, cut into thin strips
2 scallions, cut into 2-inch pieces
1/2 cup mung bean sprouts
1/2 cup bamboo shoots

garlic. Stir-fry to bring out the aroma. Turn heat up to high and add the chicken, stir-frying until it turns white. Put in the cut vegetables and continue to stir-fry for about 3 minutes or until chicken is cooked through, then add and

(continued on next page)

stir the noodles with vegetable mixture for 2 minutes. Pour sauce into the wok and keep stirring until the noodles are well-coated in sauce.

Cook's Tip: *You can make lo mein with vegetables only or use shrimp instead of chicken. Also, oyster sauce, available in bottles in the Asian food section of grocery stores, is made from oyster extracts and soy sauce. It is a very rich and dark brown sauce that adds a smoky-sweet flavor.*

Linguine with Peas and Prosciutto in a Basil Cream Sauce

This is a nice side dish that would go well with chicken or beef. Or you could serve it as a main course, along the lines of fettuccine Alfredo.

SERVES 4 TO 6

Melt the butter in a large skillet and add the diced prosciutto and garlic. Sauté for 5 minutes, until the garlic is lightly browned. Add the white wine and cook for 3 minutes. Add the lemon juice and heavy cream and cook for an additional 7 minutes or until liquid is reduced by one-third; add the peas toward the end of the cooking time. Meanwhile cook the linguine until it is al dente and drain. Add the cooked pasta to the skillet over low heat and stir well to coat evenly with the sauce. Add the grated Parmesan, season with pepper, and heat for 2 minutes more. Do not overheat. Sprinkle with the chopped basil and serve immediately.

1 tablespoon butter
6 ounces prosciutto di Parma,
    diced in 1/4-inch cubes
1 tablespoon minced garlic
1/2 cup dry white wine
1 tablespoon fresh lemon juice
1 cup heavy cream
1 cup fresh or frozen peas
1 pound dried linguine
1/2 cup freshly grated Parmesan
Pepper to taste
3 tablespoons chopped fresh basil

Cook's Tip: You can get authentic prosciutto di Parma, a cured, aged ham, in the deli sections at most grocery stores.

Mushroom Ravioli with Cream Sauce

Ravioli is enjoying a renaissance, with fillings ranging from butternut squash to lobster. This one has a rich filling of mushrooms and cream and is baked, rather than boiled in the traditional manner.

SERVES 4

In a large, heavy skillet, melt the butter and add the chopped onion; sauté until golden brown. Add garlic and fresh thyme; sauté without browning. Add the chopped mushrooms, cream, wine, and salt and pepper. Reduce until almost dry.

Turn off heat and add asiago; mix well. Check seasoning and adjust as desired. In a food processor or hand blender, puree mixture into a pulp. Allow filling to cool.

Prepare pasta dough according to package directions; if frozen, thaw. (Recipe was tested with egg roll wraps. Cut wraps into quarters.)

On each pasta square, spoon on a heaping teaspoon of filling and place another square on top. Wet fingers with water and fold over all four edges so that they stick. A 16-ounce package contains 12 wraps, enough to make 24 raviolis.

2 pounds fresh white button mushrooms, finely chopped (you can chop in food processor)
1/2 stick butter (2 ounces or 1/4 cup)
1 large Spanish or yellow onion, diced; reserve 1/4 cup for sauce recipe
1 clove garlic, minced
1/2 teaspoon chopped fresh thyme
1/2 cup heavy cream
1/2 cup white wine
Salt and pepper
3/4 cup grated Asiago
1 16-ounce package of frozen pasta sheets, available at gourmet delis or specialty stores (or wonton skins or egg roll wraps)
Olive oil
Cream Sauce (see recipe that follows)
1/4 cup grated Parmesan
Chopped Italian parsley for garnish

Place filled raviolis into two 9 × 13-inch glass baking dishes coated with olive oil. Brush additional olive oil over raviolis. Set aside and begin sauce.

Meanwhile, preheat oven to 350 degrees. Once sauce is simmering, bake raviolis for 10 minutes.

To serve, place baked raviolis on an ovenproof serving platter. Pour cream sauce over the top. Sprinkle top with the grated Parmesan and glaze under broiler until golden brown. Garnish with chopped parsley.

Cook's Tips: Although you won't be able to duplicate the restaurant's pasta per se—unless you make your own—you can buy fresh frozen pasta sheets at some of the specialty markets in town or use the refrigerated wonton or egg roll skins found in groceries.

You can boil the ravioli instead of baking. Slide raviolis into boiling water; when water returns to a boil, cook 2 minutes. Remove with slotted spoon. Transfer raviolis to ovenproof serving platter and sprinkle with Parmesan and glaze under broiler until golden brown.

Cream Sauce

MAKES 4 CUPS

In heavy pot, heat the olive oil over medium heat. Add chopped onions, garlic, dried thyme, and bay leaf; lightly sauté until onions are translucent. Turn up heat and add white wine, salt, and pepper. Reduce wine until it's almost dry. Add a quart of heavy cream and simmer until cream reduces and thickens slightly, whisking occasionally.

Strain finished sauce through a fine-meshed strainer.

2 teaspoons olive oil
1/4 cup onion, chopped
   (reserved from filling mixture)
4 cloves garlic, minced
1 pinch dried thyme
1 bay leaf
1/2 cup white wine
Salt and pepper to taste
1 quart heavy cream

Penne Mona Lisa

This easy pasta dish would make a quick, delicious dinner. Chef/owner Tom Mirabito names it for the mysterious Mona Lisa because, as he says, "I'm a romantic."

SERVES 4

In a large, heavy skillet, heat the olive oil over medium heat and sauté the garlic and shallots until transparent. Add the fresh tomatoes and red pepper flakes; sauté 2 minutes longer. Add the marinara and heavy cream and reduce slightly to thicken. Add the cooked chicken to the sauce to warm it.

Cook the penne according to package directions. Add the basil and seasonings to the sauce. When pasta is cooked, drain and stir it into the sauce.

Add Parmesan and toss. Serve.

Cook's Tip: Because this recipe calls for cooked chicken breasts and marinara sauce, you can save a lot of steps by using a store-bought rotisserie chicken and your favorite canned marinara sauce.

$1/4$ cup olive oil
$1^1/2$ tablespoons minced garlic
2 tablespoons minced shallots
1 cup diced ripe tomatoes
$1/4$ teaspoon red pepper flakes
1 cup fresh or canned marinara sauce
1 pint heavy cream
$1/2$ pound boneless, skinless chicken breasts, grilled and diced
1 pound dried penne
2 tablespoons minced fresh basil
Salt and black pepper to taste
$1/2$ cup grated Parmesan

Fettucine Alfredo

When you're looking for a quick dinner or side dish, this version of the Italian classic is ready in minutes. Café Gondolier makes its own pasta, but you can use fresh or dried.

SERVES 6 AS A MAIN DISH,
OR MORE AS A SIDE DISH

In a heavy sauce pot, scald the cream. Add the three grated cheeses, and stir over medium heat for 3 to 5 minutes, or until cheese has melted into the sauce.

Season with nutmeg and white pepper. Toss with fettuccine or pasta of your choice.

3 cups heavy whipping cream
3/4 cup grated Romano
1/2 cup grated Parmesan
1/2 cup grated provolone
Dash nutmeg
Dash white pepper
1 pound dried fettuccine,
    cooked and drained

Deluxe Macaroni and Cheese

Dazzle's General Manager Donald Rossa gave us this Macaroni and Cheese, which combines the rich flavors of fontina, Gouda, mozzarella, and smoked Cheddar. This delicious recipe is definitely not your ordinary mac 'n' cheese from a box. Serve it as a main dish or as a side with roast chicken.

SERVES 6

Bring cream and butter to a light boil. Reduce heat to medium and gradually add the cheeses, stirring until partially melted. Add the cooked macaroni and toss lightly. Continue to cook until all cheese is melted. Add salt and pepper.

Remove from heat and put into an ovenproof bowl or baking dish. Top with bread crumbs and place under broiler until topping is golden brown (about 5 minutes). Remove from oven and garnish top with tomatoes and basil.

1 1/2 cups heavy cream
1 tablespoon unsalted butter
1/4 cup shredded fontina
1/4 cup shredded Gouda
1/2 cup shredded mozzarella
1/2 cup shredded smoked Cheddar
1 pound dry macaroni, cooked and drained
Salt and pepper to taste
4 tablespoons dry bread crumbs
1 large Roma tomato, seeded and diced, for garnish
4 large leaves fresh basil, chiffonade (cut into thin strips), for garnish

Classic Macaroni and Cheese

Mel Master has one of the most happening restaurants in town. For this recipe, the chef uses signature ingredients: Smithfield ham, a special southern ham from Virginia, and Cabot cheese, an award-winning brand of Cheddar made in Vermont.

1 stick butter (4 ounces or $^1/_2$ cup)
$^3/_4$ cup flour
4 tablespoons olive oil
2 cups diced ham
1 large onion, finely diced
2 cloves garlic, minced
3 cups chilled whole milk
3 cups chilled heavy cream
3 whole bay leaves
$^1/_2$ teaspoon ground nutmeg
$^1/_2$ teaspoon ground cloves
Salt and pepper to taste
1 pound dried elbow macaroni
3 cups grated sharp white Cheddar
2 cups bread crumbs

SERVES 6 TO 8

Preheat oven to 400 degrees.

Make a roux over medium heat by melting the butter and whisking in the flour. When well mixed, cook roux for 5 minutes, until golden, not brown.

In a large saucepan over medium-high heat, add 1 tablespoon of the olive oil and the diced ham. Cook until golden brown. Remove ham and set aside.

In same pot, add onion and garlic and cook covered until onions are translucent. Add half of the roux to onion mixture and stir well to incorporate. Add the milk and cream. Whisk the mixture until lumps disappear. Add bay leaves, nutmeg, cloves, salt and pepper. Bring to a simmer, stirring frequently.

Simmer for 10 minutes. If the mixture does not start to thicken, add a bit more roux. Mixture should be thick enough to coat the back of a spoon. When mixture is thick, it is ready.

While the sauce is simmering, prepare the macaroni al dente and drain. In a large mixing bowl, combine the macaroni, ham, cheese, and the cream sauce. Mix well. Pour mixture into large baking dish. Remove bay leaves. Sprinkle the top with bread crumbs, then drizzle with 3 tablespoons olive oil.

Bake for 30 minutes or until golden.

Angel Hair Pasta with Fresh Tomatoes, Basil, and Mozzarella

Because yellow tomatoes aren't always available, I made this recipe at home with cherry tomatoes and a little fresh sautéed spinach thrown in. This is a nice, light dinner. You can buy the mozzarella balls, which are packed in liquid, at any grocery store.

MAKES 6 TO 8 servings

In a large saucepan heat the olive oil and sauté the garlic and shallots for 30 seconds.

Add the chopped tomatoes and cook for 30 more seconds. Add the tomato juice, basil, and butter and simmer until incorporated. Adjust seasonings, add the cheese and pasta, and serve.

1/4 cup olive oil
1 tablespoon minced garlic
1 tablespoon minced shallot
3 yellow tomatoes, seeded and chopped
3 red tomatoes, seeded and chopped
2 6-ounce cans tomato juice
1/2 cup julienned fresh basil
6 tablespoons butter unsalted,
  cut into pieces
1 pound fresh mozzarella balls
  (cherry-sized)
1 pound dried angel hair pasta, cooked

Rigatoni with Sausage and Tomato Cream

This dish requires substantial pasta, such as rigatoni, which is a ribbed, hollow pasta tube that will hold its shape in cooking. The sauce lightly coats rather than overwhelms the pasta. If you prefer a dish with more sauce, use less pasta, or double the sauce recipe.

SERVES 4 TO 6

Cook and drain sausage; cook pasta and drain. Sauté garlic in olive oil. Add wine to deglaze pan. Add sausage, marinara sauce, and cream and simmer on reduced heat to thicken slightly. Add Romano, basil, salt, pepper, and crushed red pepper. Toss with hot pasta and serve.

Cook's Tip: To deglaze a pan, add the wine to the pan and scrap up any browned bits with a spatula. The browned bits add flavor to the sauce.

5 ounces spicy bulk sausage
12 ounces dried rigatoni
1 teaspoon chopped garlic
1 teaspoon olive oil
1/4 cup white wine
1/2 cup homemade or canned
   marinara sauce
1/2 cup heavy cream
2 tablespoons grated Romano
2 pinches basil
2 pinches salt
2 pinches pepper
1 pinch crushed red pepper

● ●

Penne Giovanni (Ziti al Fresco)

When Restaurateur Jack Leone lived in Denver, he opened a number of wildly popular restaurants, including Café Giovanni and Al Fresco. This recipe was called either Penne Giovanni or Ziti Al Fresco, depending on which restaurant was serving it and which of the tubular pastas you use.

SERVES 10

Brown sausage until thoroughly cooked. Drain excess fat. Set aside.

Sauté onion in oil until translucent; add white wine and cook until reduced by half. Add all three kinds of tomatoes, spices and herbs, and cooked sausage and simmer over low heat until thickened, about 45 minutes. Add cream and Parmesan to tomato sauce and simmer until thick.

Cook pasta and drain. Toss pasta with sauce in pan until thoroughly coated; garnish with fresh basil and serve.

$1^1/_2$ pounds Italian sausage
1 cup diced yellow onion
1 to 2 tablespoons oil
1 cup white wine
1 14-ounce can whole peeled
    Roma tomatoes
1 14-ounce can ground Roma tomatoes
1 cup sun-dried tomatoes
1 teaspoon red pepper flakes
    (or more to taste)
1 tablespoon oregano
1 tablespoon basil
3 cups heavy cream
1 cup grated Parmesan
1 pound dried penne or ziti
Fresh basil for garnish

● ●

Baked Ziti

Without doubt, we have gotten the most requests for recipes from Racines, which is owned by Lee Goodfriend, Dixon Staples, and David Racine, owners of two other Denver landmarks, Dixons and Goodfriends. This baked ziti dish would be an easy dinner to make for the family, especially if you use a canned marinara sauce.

SERVES 6 TO 8

Preheat oven to 350 degrees.

Prepare marinara sauce and keep it hot. Blend cheeses in bowl. Cook pasta until al dente, drain, and toss lightly with olive oil. Toss pasta with marinara sauce, separate into individual baking dishes and top with blended cheeses. Bake in oven for 15 minutes until cheese is melted.

2 cups canned or homemade
  marinara sauce
$1/2$ cup crumbled goat cheese
$1/2$ cup shredded white Cheddar
$1/4$ cup freshly grated Parmesan
$1/2$ cup shredded mozzarella
12 ounces dried ziti or penne
4 tablespoons olive oil

Saffron Risotto with Shrimp

Risotto is a slow-cooked rice dish that uses Arborio, a short-grain rice that is creamy when cooked. This is an excellent all-purpose risotto that can be served as a main course or as a side dish, if you want to bypass the shrimp and substitute diced cooked carrots or other vegetables and Parmesan. Risotto is also a good recipe if you're having vegetarians over for dinner—just use vegetable broth instead of chicken and add assorted veggies. The original recipe calls for rock shrimp, but I've switched to medium shrimp, peeled and deveined, which are easier to find.

SERVES 6 TO 8

Bring broth to a simmer. On another burner, heat the wine until just warm and add powdered saffron.

Place olive oil and butter in a heavy-bottomed, high-sided pot and turn heat to medium high. Add onion and cook until it becomes translucent. Add rice. Stir rice quickly and thoroughly until completely coated with hot oil and butter mixture. The rice should become

6 cups chicken broth, low-sodium,
   if possible
1 cup dry white wine
1 teaspoon saffron, ground to a powder
   in a small mortar
2 tablespoons olive oil
2 tablespoons butter
3 tablespoons minced Spanish yellow onion
2¼ cups Arborio rice
1 pound raw medium shrimp (or 10 to 12
   ounces rock shrimp), peeled and deveined
¾ cup fresh peas, shelled and blanched,
   or frozen peas
1 tablespoon grated lemon zest (optional)
1 tablespoon chopped fresh mint (optional)

slightly toasted. Add the warm wine/saffron mixture, stirring vigorously until the wine is evaporated and the rice is flavored and colored by the saffron.

Ladle the simmering chicken broth into the rice, about a ½ cup at a time, stirring vigorously and adding more broth only as it's absorbed.

This is a slow process—if the broth is absorbed too quickly, lower the heat. Continue adding broth and stirring until rice is tender but firm to the bite and all the broth has been used. Just before you've used your last cup of broth, add the raw shrimp and frozen peas. These additions will cook as you continue to add broth and finish the dish. Add the lemon zest and mint (if desired) and remove from the heat. Adjust seasoning. Divide into serving bowls and serve at once.

Cook's Tips: The secret to a creamy risotto is adding the warmed broth a little at a time to release all the starches in the rice. This means standing over the stove for about 30 minutes, attending to the dish, so plan accordingly.

Zest is the outer peel of an orange or lemon. Use a kitchen tool called a zester (it's a little like a potato peeler) to remove the colored peel. The white pith underneath is bitter.

....

Sansone's Chez Walter Famous Carrots

Robert Sansone took over Chez Walter from former chef/owner Walter Schmuki and the name was changed to Sansone's Chez Walter. Schmuki's menu was predominantly Swiss, which Sansone has largely preserved, but as an expert chef, he also offers his own dishes. This is a tasty, slightly sweet carrot dish that's a good accompaniment to savory salmon dishes.

SERVES 6 TO 8

Place carrots in pot, cover with water, add salt. Cook on medium heat until carrots are slightly soft but still crisp, about 10 minutes. Drain half the water. To the water and carrots in the pot, add brown sugar and chicken base. Bring to a boil, cook about 1 minute, or until cube or base is dissolved. Place carrots in dish with some of the broth and sprinkle with fresh chopped dill or fresh parsley.

1 pound carrots,
   peeled and sliced $1/3$-inch thick
1 teaspoon salt
1 to 2 tablespoons brown sugar
   (or white if preferred)
1 teaspoon chicken base or bouillon,
   or to taste
Chopped fresh dill or parsley for garnish

White Corn Polenta

This was on a specialty menu at The Little Nell in Aspen, where Chef Paul Wade has turned out some wonderful dishes. Polenta is a coarsely ground cornmeal. (Do not use the already pre-pared polenta sold in tubes at the grocery.) Serve as a side dish with lamb, chicken, or beef. And although this recipe serves a crowd, it can be cut in half.

SERVES 12 (OR MORE, DEPENDING ON PORTION SIZE)

In a small amount of olive oil, cook the shal-lots and the garlic. Add stock and cream and bring to a boil. Whisk in polenta and grits, lower heat, and simmer 10 minutes. The final consistency will be that of thick oatmeal.

Add Cheddar, herbs, butter, and ancho puree. (Since the ancho adds heat, start with a $^1/_4$ cup of the ancho puree and add more to taste.)

Olive oil for cooking
$^1/_4$ cup minced shallots (4 to 5 large shallots)
$^1/_4$ cup minced garlic (4 to 5 large cloves)
$^1/_2$ gallon chicken stock
1 pint heavy cream
8 ounces white polenta or white cornmeal
3 cups hominy grits
3 cups grated Cheddar
$^1/_4$ cup chopped fresh parsley and thyme, mixed
1 stick butter (4 ounces or $^1/_2$ cup)
$^1/_2$ cup rehydrated ancho chile, pureed

Cook's Tip: Ancho chiles are dried poblanos and can range from mild to medium in heat. To make ancho puree (makes about $^1/_2$ cup): Use 2 1-ounce packages of dried ancho chiles. Rehydrate according to package instructions, drain, and remove stems. Puree in blender, adding a little water.

Eggplant with Garlic Sauce

If you're looking for a really delicious vegetable side dish, especially for a meal for company, this is it. Even eggplant-haters will love this.

SERVES 8

Heat 1 cup salad oil in wok over high heat. (Be careful when placing eggplant in hot oil; it will spatter.) Deep-fry eggplant for about 2 minutes until eggplant softens, remove eggplant with strainer, rinse with hot water, and drain. Clean wok.

Heat wok again over high heat with about 1 tablespoon of salad oil. Add garlic. When garlic is golden, put in all the vegetables, including eggplant, and stir-fry until aromatic smells rise from the pan. At that point, add Soy-Sake Sauce and cook until sauce thickens and coats vegetables. Serve hot with steamed jasmine rice.

Soy-Sake Sauce

MAKES 1 CUP

Combine all ingredients for sauce and set aside.

1 cup plus 1 tablespoon salad oil
1 Japanese eggplant, about 6 to 8 ounces, washed and cut into chunks
1 clove garlic, peeled and chopped
$1/2$ red bell pepper, seeded and cut into bite-sized pieces
2 scallions, cut into $1^1/2$-inch sections
$1/4$ jicama, peeled and cut into bite-sized pieces, about $1/8$-inch thick
Soy-Sake Sauce (see recipe that follows)

4 tablespoons low-sodium soy sauce
3 tablespoons sugar
2 tablespoons chicken broth
$1^1/2$ tablespoons rice vinegar
$1^1/2$ teaspoons sake or sherry
$1/4$ teaspoon salt
$3/4$ teaspoon chili oil
1 tablespoon sesame oil
1 tablespoon cornstarch

Baked Summer Squash Casserole

For some time, this was our number-one most requested recipe. After we finally secured the recipe, it ran in the paper—the weekend of the October blizzard some years ago. This is a standard offering on the menu at the Black-Eyed Pea, and it's easy to understand why.

SERVES 10

Wash squash, cut off tips and bad spots. Cut into 3 to 4 pieces each. Place in a stockpot, and cover with water. Place a lid on the pot and boil until tender, 15 to 20 minutes. Drain and mash.

In a large bowl, combine squash with remaining ingredients (pulse in food processor in batches, if desired, but don't overprocess—it will become gluey). Transfer into a greased 9 × 13-inch casserole dish. Bake uncovered at 350 degrees for 25 to 30 minutes or until firm. Cut in squares to serve. If you want thicker squares, bake in an 8 × 8-inch greased casserole, and increase your time accordingly.

5 pounds yellow summer squash
3 tablespoons melted butter
2 eggs
1 cup bread crumbs
1/4 cup sugar
2 tablespoons dehydrated onions
Dash of pepper

Cook's Tips: Note that the recipe calls for yellow summer squash. Although they're available all year round, the price of this squash is high in the winter and the recipe calls for 5 pounds.

This is a generous casserole: Leftovers of it can be refrigerated and reheated in a microwave oven.

Sweet Corn Custard

This recipe was served by former Panzano chef Jennifer Jasinski in quarter-sized portions on an appetizer plate. Unlike standard corn custards, this one is strained, so it's very smooth and it's made in custard cups or ramekins.

SERVES 4

Preheat oven to 300 degrees.

Lightly butter four 6-ounce ramekins. Put the corn kernels and heavy cream together in a heavy-bottomed sauce pot. Simmer on low until the corn is tender, about 15 to 20 minutes. (If using frozen corn, simmer on low for 5 to 10 minutes.)

Puree the cream mixture in a blender until smooth. Season the mixture with salt and white pepper. Strain the corn-cream mixture through a fine sieve into a stainless-steel bowl.

In a separate bowl, crack the eggs and whisk briefly. Slowly temper the eggs by adding a few tablespoons of the hot cream mixture to the eggs to raise their temperature (without cooking or curdling the eggs); then whisk eggs into remaining liquid.

> $1^1/_2$ cups fresh corn kernels
>   (2 to 3 ears fresh corn) or frozen corn
> 1 cup heavy cream
> 2 large eggs
> $^1/_4$ teaspoon salt
> $^1/_8$ teaspoon white pepper

Place the ramekins in a baking dish, large enough to fill with water to surround ramekins. (This is called a bain-marie or water bath method of cooking: The surrounding hot water prevents curdling of such delicate dishes as custards.) Carefully pour the cream mixture into the ramekins and pour hot water into the baking dish so that water comes halfway up the sides of the ramekins. Cover the baking dish with foil, and poke holes in the foil so the steam will vent but the tops of the custards won't color.

Bake 60 to 75 minutes. The custards are done when you jiggle them and they stay set.

Remove from the water bath and serve in ramekins.

Grilled Mixed Vegetables

Grilled and roasted vegetables have become a popular accompaniment for any meal. In this case, Chef Mark Johnson tosses the vegetables with olive oil mixed with garlic for some extra flavor. Any combination of vegetables will work.

APPROXIMATELY $1/3$ POUND
OF VEGETABLES PER SERVING

Leave the mushrooms whole and cut tomatoes only in half. Cut remaining vegetables into pieces $1/4$- to $1/2$-inch thick—large enough so they won't fall through the spaces on the grill. In a large mixing bowl, gently toss vegetables with oil and garlic. Add kosher salt and pepper to taste. Gently toss again and place on a hot grill. Grill one side for about 2 minutes, then turn with tongs and cook to desired firmness. Some vegetables will cook faster than others, so monitor carefully. If you prefer, skewer vegetables for easier turning on the grill.

Suggested vegetables: zucchini; yellow squash; portobello mushrooms; eggplant; bell peppers (any color); carrots (blanch for about 1 minute); onions; fennel; cremini mushrooms; tomatoes

$1/2$ to 1 cup extra virgin olive oil, depending on amount of vegetables

$1/2$ to 1 tablespoon minced garlic (amount per your preference)

Kosher salt to taste

Freshly ground pepper to taste

Cook's Tip: If you prefer to roast the vegetables, place them in a pan and roast at 450 degrees until vegetables are soft. Any sliced vegetables should be sliced to an even thickness and blanch harder vegetables such as carrots so that the vegetables will finish evenly.

Frijoles a la Charra

The owners of the Black-Eyed Pea restaurant chain spread their wings by opening Hacienda Colorado.

SERVES 8

Place the beans in a heavy, deep pot. Cover in cold water and soak overnight. After soaking, drain and rinse the beans. Add 3 quarts fresh water and $1/2$ teaspoon salt and cook the beans at a low boil for 2 to 3 hours until tender.

In a separate pan, sauté the bacon until it is crispy. Remove the bacon and discard (or save for another recipe), reserving the bacon grease in the pan. Add the diced onions and sauté until translucent.

Once the beans are tender, add the onions and their grease to the bean pot. Stir in salt to

> $1^1/2$ pounds dried pinto beans
> 3 quarts water
> 1 to $1^1/2$ teaspoons salt
> $3/4$ pound smoked bacon
> 1 large white onion, diced
> $1/2$ to 1 teaspoon salt
> $1/2$ teaspoon garlic powder
> 2 cups diced tomatoes
> 3 tablespoons chopped fresh cilantro

taste—about $1/2$ to 1 teaspoon, and garlic powder. Continue cooking the beans on low heat for another 20 minutes.

Add the diced tomatoes and fresh cilantro and stir. Beans are ready to serve, or can be covered and kept on low heat until needed. Serve in a bowl with tortillas on the side, or over rice.

- -

Red and Green Lentil Salad

The Market makes many wonderful, healthy salads, including this lentil salad, made with green lentils, red peppers, celery, and cilantro. This recipe reminds me of making guacamole, where you can add more or less cilantro or seasonings to suit your tastes.

SERVES 8 TO 10

Combine lentils and water in a pot and place over high heat. Bring to a boil and cook at a simmer until lentils are cooked through, about 30 minutes. Do not overcook. Drain water.

Mix vegetables with lemon juice and olive oil; add lentils and toss well. Adjust seasonings to your taste.

2 cups dried green lentils, washed and sorted
1 quart water
2 green onions, diced
2 celery stalks, diced
1 bell pepper, red or green, diced
2 tomatoes, diced
$1/4$ cup chopped cilantro, or to taste
2 whole canned pimientos, drained and diced
$1/2$ red onion, diced
$1/4$ cup fresh lemon juice
$1/2$ cup olive oil
Salt to taste
Red crushed pepper to taste

- -

Balsamic Lentils

Although I've never been a fan of lentils, this dish is delicious. Chef Matt Selby of the Vesta Dipping Grill uses balsamic vinegar and soy sauce to give the lentils punch. This dish is also good served over steamed basmati rice.

SERVES 8 TO 10

Combine lentils and water in a sauce pot and place over high heat. Bring to a boil and cook until lentils are cooked through, approximately 30 minutes. Drain water. Mix in balsamic vinegar and soy sauce, up to 1 cup of each (in equal amounts), depending on your preferences. Serve hot, topped with butter.

2 cups dried brown lentils
  (washed and sorted)
1 quart water
1 cup balsamic vinegar or to taste
1 cup soy sauce or to taste
1 tablespoon butter

Desserts

(continued on next page)

Desserts, *continued*

Semisweet Chocolate Brownies with Banana Caramel Sauce

This is a very rich, very moist fudgy chocolate brownie. In the words of one of my teenage tasters: These are positively addictive. The ice cream and Banana Caramel Sauce are strictly optional—a way to dress up the brownies for company, if desired.

MAKES 1 9 × 13-INCH PAN

Preheat oven to 350 degrees.

In the top of a double boiler, melt chocolates and butter over simmering water. Place eggs, sugar, sour cream, and vanilla in bowl; whisk to combine. When the chocolate is melted and has cooled slightly, combine with egg mixture, whipping with a wire whisk to blend. Add flour and mix.

Pour batter into a greased 9 × 13-inch pan. Bake for 20 to 30 minutes, until brownie is

5 ounces semisweet chocolate
5 ounces unsweetened chocolate
2 sticks butter ($1/2$ pound or 1 cup)
4 eggs
2 cups sugar
$1/6$ cup sour cream
2 teaspoons vanilla extract
$1/2$ cup flour
Vanilla ice cream
Banana Caramel Sauce
  (see recipe that follows)

firm and a toothpick inserted in center comes out clean. Cool in pan on wire rack and cut into squares.

Serve by topping brownie with vanilla ice cream. Serve Banana Caramel Sauce on the side.

Banana Caramel Sauce

MAKES $1/2$ CUP

$1/2$ cup brown sugar
$1/2$ cup rum
2 just-ripe bananas, halved lengthwise
4 tablespoons butter

Mix brown sugar and rum together. In a separate pan, sauté bananas in 4 tablespoons butter until soft, about 1 to 2 minutes. Add brown sugar and rum combination and reduce to syrup consistency. Rum can be extremely volatile, although mixing it with the brown sugar will make it less likely to flame. Nevertheless, be careful when cooking.

. . . .

Frosted Brownies

These brownies can be even more decadent when paired with ice cream and hot fudge sauce.

MAKES 1 8-INCH SQUARE PAN

Preheat oven to 350 degrees.

Melt one stick of butter with the unsweetened chocolate in the top of a double boiler over simmering water. Let cool. Cream the remaining stick of butter with sugar. Mix together the salt and cake flour. Add the eggs to the creamed mixture slowly and blend until smooth. Next, add flour. Finally, add the melted chocolate mixture, the vanilla and the chopped walnuts and fold in by hand with a rubber spatula.

Spray sides and bottom of an 8-inch square pan. Pour the brownie mixture into the pan and spread out evenly with your spatula. Bake for 30 to 40 minutes. You may also use a 9 × 13-inch pan, but brownies will be thinner; lessen your time accordingly.

2 sticks unsalted butter
  ($1/2$ pound or 1 cup), softened
4 ounces unsweetened chocolate
2 cups sugar
$1^1/2$ teaspoons salt
1 cup cake flour
3 eggs
1 teaspoon vanilla extract
$3/4$ cup chopped walnuts
12 walnut halves
2 to 4 ounces semisweet chocolate,
  depending on your preference

Cool in pan on wire rack and cut into 12 servings. Top each brownie with a walnut half and drizzle with melted semisweet chocolate. Serve cold or warm with ice cream and hot fudge sauce.

Recipe can be doubled. Use a 12 × 16 × 1-inch pan.

. . . .

Chocolate Chip Cookies

Years ago, chef/co-owner Michael Bortz of Palmetto Grille sold fabulous chocolate chip cookies at the restaurant and bakery. In testing the recipe at home and bringing the results to work, I found that there are two camps of chocolate chip cookie lovers—crispy or chewy. Bortz's cookies are really crispy, which is difficult to do at home with cookies this large, unless you have a convection oven.

I'll take either crispy or chewy, but I lean toward chewy. Using his recipe, I made the cookies megasize, like he does, and baked them longer at a lower temperature, which produced a wonderful chewy cookie. You can use semisweet or milk chocolate chips, depending on your preference. My kids will tell you that this is one of their favorite recipes.

MAKES 12 VERY LARGE COOKIES

Preheat oven to 325 degrees.

Cream butter and sugars. Add eggs and vanilla. Mix baking soda, salt, and flour together. Add to batter and mix well. Stir in chocolate chips.

2 sticks butter ($^1/_2$ pound or 1 cup), softened
$1^1/_2$ cups dark brown sugar, firmly packed
$^1/_2$ cup sugar
2 eggs
1 teaspoon vanilla extract
1 teaspoon baking soda
1 teaspoon salt
3 cups all-purpose flour
12 ounces semisweet or milk chocolate chips

Roll into 12 balls. You may only fit a few cookies on the sheet at one time. Bake 12 to 14 minutes on an ungreased cookie sheet. If cookies look too raw, add time in 1-minute increments. Cookies can also be made smaller, if desired. Check for doneness at 10 minutes for these. Remove from oven, let sit for a few minutes, and cool cookies on racks.

Pumpkin Chocolate Chip Cookies

Who would have guessed that my kids would love these large, soft pumpkin chocolate chip cookies? (At least we're sneaking in a vegetable, next to that chocolate.)

MAKES 1½ DOZEN 3-INCH COOKIES

Preheat oven to 300 degrees.

Cream butter with sugar. Beat until fluffy. Blend in pumpkin, egg, and vanilla. Mixture will look slightly curdled.

In another bowl, sift together flour, baking soda, baking powder, cinnamon, nutmeg, and salt. Stir into butter mixture and blend well. Fold in chocolate chips. Do not overmix.

Using a large ice cream scoop, scoop cookies onto ungreased baking sheet. Do not crowd cookies on sheet; cookies will spread.

Bake at 300 degrees around 22 to 24 minutes. Remove from oven, let sit on cookie sheet for a minute or so, then place cookies on racks to cool.

1 stick butter (4 ounces or ½ cup)
1½ cups sugar
1 cup canned pumpkin
1 egg
1 teaspoon vanilla extract
2½ cups flour
1 teaspoon baking soda
¾ teaspoon baking powder
1 teaspoon cinnamon
1 teaspoon nutmeg
¼ teaspoon salt
¾ cup chocolate chips

Cook's Tip: The secret to these soft cookies is baking at a low temperature.

Lemon Squares

Years ago my aunt baked a batch of lemon squares for the holiday and I fell in love with the buttery crust and lemony, not-too-tart taste. In Denver, Patti and Lisa Miller, in-laws and co-owners of Pasta, Pasta, Pasta, have made their version a must-have.

MAKES 1 11 × 17-INCH PAN

Preheat oven to 350 degrees.

To make the crust: Melt the butter. Add 4 cups flour and 1 cup sugar to make a dough. Press into the bottom of a very well-greased 11 × 17-inch pan. Bake 15 to 20 minutes until slightly brown. Set aside while you make the filling.

To make the filling: Whisk together eggs, $1/2$ cup flour, 3 cups sugar, and lemon juice and pour over baked crust. Bake another 20 minutes. Do not overbake. Bars will firm up as they cool. To serve, sprinkle with powdered sugar, if desired.

4 sticks butter (1 pound or 2 cups)
$4^1/2$ cups flour
4 cups sugar
8 eggs
Juice from 3 to 4 lemons
Powdered sugar (optional)

Cook's Tip: You'll find that the bars tend to come out of the pan easier when thoroughly cooled. Obviously, these are very rich with 4 sticks of butter in the crust alone, but they feed a crowd. Use an 11 × 17-inch sheet pan or pan of similar size. We tried cutting the recipe in half and using a 9 × 13-inch pan. It works in a pinch, but there is a distinct difference in taste and texture.

Brown Palace Hotel Macaroons

Next to the Brown Palace scones, the hotel's macaroons are probably the best-known teatime treat at the Brown Palace. Although macaroons can be a coconut-based cookie, authentic French macaroons are made with ground almonds.

MAKES ABOUT 36 COOKIES

Preheat oven to 350 degrees.

Line cookie sheet with parchment paper. Combine almond paste and both sugars in a mixing bowl with a paddle attachment. Mix until it becomes a coarse meal texture. Slowly add egg whites until incorporated and smooth. Place mixture into a piping bag with a No. 7 or No. 8 round tip and pipe to the size of a quarter onto the cookie sheet. If you do not have a piping bag, drop by rounded teaspoon onto cookie sheet. Cookies should be about quarter size.

14 ounces almond paste
$5/8$ cup sugar
$5/8$ cup powdered sugar
$1/2$ cup egg whites
(whites from about 3 eggs)

After piping or spooning, press down cookie very slightly with the back of a spoon. Sprinkle with additional sugar, if desired. Bake for 9 to 11 minutes; do not overbake. Cookies should be crisp, but not dry.

Cook's Tips: Prepared almond paste usually comes in a tube and is found in the baking aisle of the grocery stores. You'll want to use parchment paper, available at most grocery stores and gourmet kitchenware stores, so that the cookies do not stick to the pan.

Ginger Cookies

These sweetly spiced treats are a nice dessert at the end of a heavy meal. Baking a batch is a (ginger) snap.

MAKES ABOUT 36 COOKIES

Cream butter and sugar until well blended. Add egg and molasses and mix well. Sift together dry ingredients (except sugar for dipping). Add egg mixture to dry mixture and mix well.

Roll dough into 1-inch diameter balls and dip in granulated sugar. Bake on slightly greased cookie sheet at 350 degrees for 12 minutes. Remove from oven and cool on wire racks.

$1^1/_2$ sticks butter (12 ounces or $^3/_4$ cup), softened
1 cup brown sugar, packed
1 egg
$^1/_4$ cup molasses
2 cups flour
$^1/_4$ teaspoon salt
1 teaspoon baking powder
$^1/_2$ teaspoon ground cloves
$^1/_2$ teaspoon ground cinnamon
1 teaspoon ground ginger
Granulated sugar for dipping the cookies

Gingerbread

If you've only had that cafeteria favorite, a square of gingerbread with the fake whipped cream on top, you're in for a real treat with this recipe, which is made with grated gingerroot and a potpourri of spices.

MAKES 1 9 × 13-INCH CAKE

Preheat oven to 325 degrees.

Grease cake pan, lining the bottom with parchment paper. In a small saucepan, bring water and baking soda to a boil. Set aside.

In a small mixing bowl, sift together flour, cinnamon, baking powder, cloves, and salt. Set aside.

In a medium-sized bowl, cream butter and sugar and beat until very light and fluffy. Add molasses, ginger, and lemon zest to butter and sugar. Beat well, scraping down the sides of the bowl with a rubber scraper to make sure everything is well combined.

Add the flour mixture and hot water and soda alternately, a third at a time, mixing very well between each addition, and again scraping the sides of the bowl.

Finally, add eggs and mix thoroughly.

$1^1/_2$ cups water
$^1/_2$ tablespoon baking soda
3 cups all-purpose flour
2 teaspoons cinnamon
$1^1/_2$ teaspoons baking powder
$^1/_2$ teaspoon ground cloves
$^1/_4$ teaspoon salt
1 stick butter (4 ounces or $^1/_2$ cup), softened
1 cup sugar
1 cup molasses
2 tablespoons peeled and finely grated gingerroot
Zest of $^1/_2$ lemon (grated peel), finely chopped
2 eggs

Bake for 38 to 40 minutes, or until a toothpick inserted in center comes out clean. Cool in the pan on a wire rack. Gingerbread may be served warm.

Cook's Tip: Fresh gingerroot and dried ginger powder are not interchangeable. To use fresh ginger, choose a root that feels firm and use a knife to peel the brown skin. Grate on a handheld grater.

Apple Crostata

This superb rustic apple tart takes all the guesswork out of the drama (and for some, trauma) of making an apple pie. You place the piecrust on a cookie sheet, put the filling on top, and crimp the dough around the edges in a free-form style. There is no right or wrong in shaping this tart—the less perfect the folds of the crust dough, the better.

SERVES 8 TO 10

Prepare Tart Crust as directed and refrigerate dough.

In a large sauté pan, melt the butter until foaming and add the sugar. Cook about 2 minutes until light brown, and add the apples. Cook until apples are slightly soft, give up their juices and liquid becomes syrupy again. Add the spices, mixing well. Add the cornstarch and water mixture and mix well, cooking 1 minute.

Remove filling and cool completely.

Preheat oven to 350 degrees.

Next, roll out crust dough into a 9-inch circle on a lightly floured surface with a floured rolling pin; place on a baking sheet. Scoop

Tart Crust (see recipe that follows)
3 to 4 Granny Smith apples, peeled, cored and sliced, or 3 apples plus 2 peaches, peeled, cored and pitted, and sliced
1/2 stick butter (2 ounces or 1/4 cup)
1/2 cup superfine sugar
3/4 teaspoon cinnamon
1/2 teaspoon nutmeg
1 tablespoon cornstarch dissolved in 1 tablespoon water
Heavy cream as needed
Coarse sugar for coating crust (optional)

apple filling into center of dough, leaving an ample border of dough. Overlap folds of dough around the filling, using about 8 folds in all to result in a 4-inch opening in the center of the fruit tart.

Brush the crust with heavy cream. Sprinkle crust with sugar, if desired.

Bake in oven until browned and crisped, about 35 to 40 minutes.

(continued on next page)

Tart Crust

MAKES 1

With a knife or pastry blender, cut the butter into 1/4-inch cubes and keep cold.

Mix flour, sugar, and salt together. Add the butter to the dry ingredients, using a food processor if available (if not, continue using pastry blender). Pulse until mixture is in small pieces. Add the ice water and mix very briefly (too much mixing will make it tough). Stop be-

2 sticks chilled butter (1/2 pound or 1 cup)
2 cups all-purpose flour
1/3 cup superfine sugar
1/2 teaspoon salt
1/4 cup ice water

fore the dough is a solid mass. (It's better to leave it a little crumbly.) Press the dough together and form into a ball. Place ball on sheet of plastic wrap; flatten ball slightly, wrap, and refrigerate at least 1 hour.

Wolfgang Puck's Grand Café Oatmeal Apple Streusel Crisp Tartlets

This dessert is the Denver restaurant's adaptation of a recipe from one of Wolfgang Puck's cookbooks.

This recipe is reprinted with the kind permission of Wolfgang Puck, who retains all rights to it.

MAKES 8 4-INCH TARTLETS

Roll the Sugar Dough into two 11-inch squares. Put each on parchment paper and stack on a tray. Cover with parchment and chill in refrigerator for 20 minutes.

Cut dough into eight 5-inch circles and fit each into a 4-inch tartlet tin or ramekin. If necessary, you can re-roll the dough trimmings to make more 5-inch circles.

Preheat oven to 325 degrees.

Peel, core, and slice apples 1/4-inch thick. Melt the butter in a large sauté pan over medium heat. Add apples and sprinkle with sugar. Cook until sugar caramelizes but apples retain their crunchiness, about 10 minutes.

Remove sauté pan from heat and pour brandy over apples, briefly allowing liquor to warm in

Sugar Dough (see recipe that follows)
8 small cooking apples (Pippin, Granny Smith, or Golden Delicious)
4 tablespoons unsalted butter
1/2 cup sugar
1/4 cup Calvados or another apple brandy (you may need a little more if it won't ignite)
Streusel (see recipe that follows)
Caramel Sauce (see recipe that follows)
8 scoops vanilla ice cream

the mixture. Carefully ignite the brandied apples (you may need a bit more brandy if it doesn't light) and allow the flame to die out. Set pan aside to cool.

Spoon apple mixture into the unbaked tart shells. Top each tartlet with the Streusel mixture. Bake for 40 to 45 minutes until streusel is golden brown.

Pour Caramel Sauce on dessert plate and place tartlet in the center. Serve with a scoop of ice cream alongside tartlet.

(continued on next page)

Cook's Tips: For the Sugar Dough, if you want to attempt to measure the flour in cups, 2 cups of sifted flour weighs about 8$^{1}/_{2}$ ounces. Also, dough may be made in a food processor, but divide it into two batches for best results.

For the Streusel, you'll have leftover topping after covering all 8 tartlets. Leftover topping can be used to top baked apples or muffins.

Sugar Dough

MAKES CRUSTS FOR 8 4-INCH TARTLETS

Cut butter into chunks (not larger than a tablespoon) and place in a large mixing bowl.

Add the two flours, salt, and sugar. Mix on low speed with a dough hook until the butter is evenly distributed throughout the flour.

Add the yolks and cream. Continue to mix on low speed until the dough pulls away from the sides of the bowl. (This takes about 15 minutes, so stay with it.) Remove the dough and divide into two equal pieces, flattening each into a 6-inch round. Wrap each round in plastic wrap and chill in refrigerator for at least 2 hours, or overnight.

2$^{1}/_{2}$ sticks unsalted butter (10 ounces or 1$^{1}/_{4}$ cups), slightly softened
8 ounces pastry flour (buy in bulk; use a scale)
8 ounces all-purpose flour (buy in bulk; use a scale)
1 pinch of salt
$^{1}/_{2}$ cup sugar
2 egg yolks
1$^{1}/_{2}$ tablespoons heavy cream

Streusel

MAKES TOPPING FOR 8
4-INCH TARTLETS

Combine dry ingredients with a fork. Cut in the butter gradually with pastry blender or knives, until mixture resembles very coarse meal. Refrigerate.

> $2/3$ cup all-purpose flour
> 1 cup uncooked rolled oats
> 1 cup brown sugar, packed
> 1 teaspoon ground cinnamon
> $1/2$ teaspoon salt
> 6 tablespoons unsalted butter, chopped

Caramel Sauce

MAKES ENOUGH FOR 8
4-INCH TARTLETS

Combine the water and sugar in a small saucepan and bring to a boil. Cook gently until the liquid is thickened and a deep golden brown. Remove pan from heat and slowly whisk in the cream. Be careful—cream may splash up when you pour it into the hot syrup. Whisk until smooth.

> 1 cup sugar
> $1/2$ cup water
> $1/3$ cup heavy cream

Black Bottom Pie

Black Bottom Pie has been a staple at the Brown Palace since the turn of the century.

MAKES 2 9-INCH PIES

Over medium heat, bring milk, half-and-half, sugar, and vanilla bean just to a boil in large saucepan. Meanwhile, whisk together the eggs, vanilla extract, and cornstarch until smooth.

Turn off heat under pan and remove the vanilla bean. Gradually pour half the hot milk mixture into the egg mixture and whisk quickly so as not to scramble the eggs. Incorporate that mixture back into the hot milk mixture on the stove and whisk quickly over medium heat as it thickens. Return to a boil for 1 minute, still whisking. (Careful—it will splatter a bit.)

Cover bottom of each prebaked pie shell with $1/2$ cup chocolate and divide the custard between both pies. (The chocolate needs to be finely chopped and spread evenly over the

2 cups milk
2 cups half-and-half
1 cup sugar
$1/2$ vanilla bean, split lengthwise
2 eggs
1 tablespoon vanilla extract
$1/2$ cup cornstarch
2 pie shells, prebaked and cooled
Whipped cream for garnish
12 ounces dark semisweet chocolate,
   very finely chopped
   (mini-morsels can also be used)

bottom of the pies. Otherwise, once the pie cools, the chocolate will harden into a thick clump.) Cover custard with plastic wrap and cool in refrigerator. Serve slightly chilled.

To serve, top with whipped cream and $1/4$ cup of finely chopped chocolate for each pie.

Wolfgang Puck's Grand Café Key Lime Pie

Key lime pie has always been popular, but in the last couple years, key limes, a small variety of lime grown in Florida, have shown up at the grocery store. Key limes are more delicate and flavorful than the common Persian lime. Do not substitute. Note that the recipe uses a homemade graham cracker crust. Plan ahead because the key lime filling takes more than an hour to bake and then needs to be chilled.

This recipe is reprinted with the kind permission of Wolfgang Puck, who retains all rights to it.

MAKES 1 10-INCH PIE

Preheat oven to 300 degrees.

To make the crust: Combine graham cracker crumbs, melted butter, and brown sugar in a stainless-steel bowl, mix well. Press into a 10-inch glass pie pan to about $1/4$-inch thickness.

To make the filling: Mix egg yolks with sweetened condensed milk. Add lime juice and stir until completely combined. Pour into prepared pie shell and bake for approximately 1 hour to 1 hour, 15 minutes. Custard should be slightly firm to the touch. Cool, cover with plastic wrap, and chill in refrigerator.

1$1/2$ cups graham cracker crumbs
    (about 10 full-size graham crackers)
1 stick melted butter ($1/4$ pound)
$1/3$ cup brown sugar
10 egg yolks
2 cups sweetened condensed milk
1$1/2$ cups key lime juice or
    (about) 2 pounds key limes, juiced
1 cup egg whites
2 cups granulated sugar

Cook's Tip: If you can't find key limes, you can use Nellie & Joe's Key Lime Juice, which is available at the grocery stores.

To make the meringue: Place egg whites and sugar in a mixing bowl of an electric mixer. Place bowl over a saucepan with boiling water, as you would a double boiler (bowl should not be in the water). You can also pour egg white and sugar into the top of a double boiler, then later put in mixing bowl to whip (or use handheld mixer). Heat whites, stirring with a whisk until they are hot to the touch, about 120 degrees.

(continued on next page)

Preheat oven to 500 degrees.

Remove bowl from saucepan with water. Place whip attachment on electric mixer and whip on high speed until whites form stiff peaks and are cool.

Daub any moisture on top of chilled pie with paper towel. Top with whipped meringue, being sure to cover completely, and bake in hot oven until meringue is very lightly browned (2 to 3 minutes—watch carefully).

Strawberry Mascarpone Tart

Former Panzano Chef Jennifer Jasinski originally created this sophisticated dessert using tart shells of the sweetened short pastry called pâte sucrée. To ease the preparation, however, you may use any pastry recipe for tarts or store-bought tart shells. The end result? A dessert that is creamy, smooth, and a little tart.

MAKES 8 4-INCH
TART-SIZE PASTRY SHELLS

$^1/_2$ pound mascarpone
1 cup plus 1 tablespoon sugar
1 teaspoon freshly grated orange zest (peel)
$^1/_2$ cup heavy cream
$1^1/_2$ teaspoons vanilla extract
2 pints strawberries
$1^1/_4$ cups balsamic vinegar
8 4-inch tart-size pastry shells,
   store-bought, or Sugar Dough recipe
   on page 198, or similar, prebaked
Fresh mint sprigs for garnish

To prepare the mascarpone cream: Combine the mascarpone, 3 tablespoons sugar, orange zest, cream, and vanilla. Whisk until they are combined. Be careful not to overmix or the cream will separate. Cover and refrigerate until needed.

To prepare the strawberries: Wash and cut the stems off the strawberries. Place the strawberries in a bowl. In a separate bowl, whisk together 2 tablespoons sugar and $^1/_4$ cup balsamic vinegar until the sugar dissolves. Pour the mixture over the strawberries. Cover and refrigerate for up to 2 hours (this time allows the sugar and berries to macerate or for flavors to meld).

To prepare the balsamic reduction: Combine remaining 1 cup balsamic vinegar and $^1/_2$ cup sugar in a small saucepan and bring to a low boil.

Simmer until the mixture has reduced by half. Cool and keep the syrup at room temperature.

To assemble the tarts: Place a baked shell on each serving plate. Fill each shell with $^1/_3$ to $^1/_2$ cup of the mascarpone mixture. You may do this with a spoon or by placing the cream in a pastry bag and piping it into the shell. Place 5 to 7 balsamic strawberries with their tips pointing upward on top of the mascarpone cream. Drizzle the balsamic reduction over the tops of each assembled tart. Make sure that the balsamic reduction overlaps the edges of the tart and is drizzled on the plate (use sparingly). Finish each with a sprig of fresh mint.

To-Die-For Strawberry Pie

Sam Arnold, western food expert and raconteur, built his restaurant in Morrison as a replica of Bent's Fort. He has written a number of cookbooks, including *The Fort Cookbook*, filled with his authentic, often historical, and always inventive recipes. This pie is light and flavorful and would be perfect in the summertime or as a nice finish to a heavy meal. It is easy to make, but it takes a couple hours to set up in the refrigerator.

MAKES 1 9-INCH PIE

Puree 1/2 cup sliced strawberries with lime juice in a blender or food processor, then mix in condensed milk. Pour into a bowl, and stir in the remaining sliced strawberries and almond extract and mix. Pour mixture into the prepared pie shell and refrigerate. Pie will need at least 2 hours or longer to set up.

Just before serving, whip cream, adding rum flavoring and powdered sugar as it thickens. Continue whipping until soft peaks form. Cover the top of the pie with a thick layer of whipped cream. Garnish by placing whole strawberries around the outside of the pie, with one strawberry in the middle.

2 cups sliced strawberries (about 1 pound)
1/3 cup fresh lime juice (about 3 limes)
1 14-ounce can sweetened condensed milk
1/2 teaspoon almond extract
1 store-bought 9-inch graham cracker crust, or use crust recipe on page 201
1 cup whipping cream
1 teaspoon dark rum flavoring (optional)
2 tablespoons powdered sugar
Whole strawberries for garnish

Cook's Tip: Use fresh-squeezed lime juice and not the concentrated bottled juice or plastic squeeze limes for this recipe.

Chocolate Cheesecake

This is a creamy, not too chocolaty cheesecake. And yes, it does call for a dozen eggs. Note that the cheesecake should be refrigerated overnight.

MAKES 1 10-INCH CHEESECAKE

Mix together graham cracker crumbs, melted butter, and $1/2$ cup each sugar and brown sugar in a bowl. Set aside.

Soften cream cheese in electric mixer. Add vanilla, flour, and sugar; mix and scrape down sides of bowl to ensure that everything is well combined. Add sour cream; mix and scrape sides of bowl again. Add eggs a little at a time, mixing and scraping down sides of bowl, until eggs are incorporated in the batter. Melt chocolate and cool slightly. Add some of the cheesecake batter to the chocolate to lighten it and then add chocolate mixture back to remaining batter in mixer. Mix until well blended.

Preheat oven to 325 degrees.

1$1/2$ cups graham cracker or Oreo crumbs
1 stick butter ($1/4$ pound or $1/2$ cup), melted
A scant $1/2$ cup sugar
A scant $1/2$ cup brown sugar
1$1/2$ pounds cream cheese
1 teaspoon vanilla extract
$1/2$ cup flour
1$3/4$ cups sugar
1 cup sour cream
12 eggs
6 ounces semisweet chocolate

Grease sides and bottom of a 10-inch springform pan and press graham cracker crumb mixture into bottom of pan. Pour in cheesecake batter. Bake in a water bath (place pan in a larger pan that is filled with hot water that comes $3/4$ of the way up the sides of the 10-inch pan). Bake for 60 to 75 minutes or until cheesecake is firm to the touch and a toothpick comes out clean. Do not overbake. Cool. Cover lightly with foil and refrigerate overnight.

Warm Bittersweet Chocolate Cupcakes

Kevin Taylor became so well-known for these bittersweet chocolate cupcakes iced with a rich ganache that they have become one of his signature desserts.

MAKES 8 CUPCAKES

Preheat oven to 350 degrees.

Bring $1/2$ cup cream, cocoa powder, and butter to a boil. Remove from heat; stir in 5 ounces chopped chocolate until melted. Stir in vanilla.

In a heavy-duty electric mixer, whip eggs with sugar until thick and lightened in color and batter falls from beaters ribbonlike, about 6 minutes. Gently fold in chocolate mixture and pecans. (Do not overmix.) Grease muffin pans. Most muffin pans accommodate 6 cupcakes; if this is the case for you, you'll need to use two pans. If so, it's best to use 4 cups out of each pan (a pan with fewer cupcakes will bake much faster, so this will even the cooking time). Sprinkle with sugar. Fill cups two-thirds full with batter. Bake for 12 to 15 minutes, until toothpick comes out clean. Allow to cool in pan for 10 minutes; turn upside down to remove cupcakes.

$3/4$ cup heavy cream, divided
1 tablespoon cocoa powder
2 tablespoons butter
7 ounces chopped Callebaut bittersweet chocolate, divided
1 teaspoon vanilla extract
2 eggs
$1/4$ cup granulated sugar, plus extra for cupcake pans
$1/4$ cup ground pecans

To make ganache (a French term for any combination of chocolate and cream, whether for frosting, glaze, or filling), bring $1/4$ cup cream to a boil. Remove from heat; stir in remaining 2 ounces chocolate until melted. Set aside until just warm, stirring occasionally to prevent skin from forming. Spoon warm ganache over each cupcake. Serve cupcakes warm with ice cream or whipped cream.

Chef's Tip: These are very fragile and light textured rather than cake-y and they should be served warm. I would put each cupcake on a plate and spoon the ganache over it.

Espresso Pound Cake

With five full-time bakers, it's no wonder this bakery/coffee shop is offering up some fabulous treats. Because the Espresso Pound Cake was cut down from a four-batch size and baking can be so tricky, I had trouble getting it to work well in the home kitchen. After consulting with owner Tammy Davis, I added sour cream to the recipe and that did the trick. It's moist and delicious and would taste great with a scoop of coffee ice cream for dessert. It's also a nice breakfast cake. If you allow the flavors to meld overnight, the cake tastes even better the next day.

MAKES 1 9 × 5-INCH LOAF PAN

Preheat to 325 degrees.

Cream together the butter and sugar, until fluffy, about 3 to 4 minutes, with electric mixer. Add espresso powder and beat in 1 egg at a time until all 6 are incorporated. Add the brewed espresso. Mix. Add the sour cream.

In a separate bowl, mix cake flour, salt, baking powder, and baking soda together. Add to batter and mix until well blended. Pour into greased loaf pan.

2 sticks butter ($1/2$ pound or 1 cup), softened
$1^1/2$ cups sugar
1 tablespoon instant espresso powder
6 eggs
3 ounces brewed espresso
$3/4$ cup sour cream
$2^1/4$ cups cake flour
$1/2$ teaspoon salt
$3/4$ teaspoon baking powder
$1/4$ teaspoon baking soda

Bake for 30 minutes; rotate pan and bake another 30 minutes. Test with a toothpick; if it does not come out clean, continue baking and check every 5 to 10 minutes until done. Total cooking time should be 60 to 75 minutes; do not overbake. Cool.

Cook's Tip: *Instant espresso powder is available in groceries and specialty stores, usually in the instant coffee aisle. To make the brewed espresso, you add the powder to boiling water per the product directions.*

Chocolate Velvet Pound Cake

As with the Espresso Pound Cake (see page 207), I tweaked the ingredients with sour cream to make the recipe work better at home.

MAKES 1 9 × 5-INCH LOAF

Preheat oven to 375 degrees.

Cream the butter and the sugar. Add the vanilla and the eggs, one at a time, beating well after each addition. Add the sour cream.

In a medium bowl, whisk the cocoa powder, the cake flour, the baking powder, and the salt. Add half of the chocolate mixture to the batter in the bowl and mix. Add the boiling water and mix. Add the remaining chocolate mixture and beat for about 1 minute to aerate the batter and to develop its structure.

Scrape down the sides of the bowl to mix thoroughly. Scrape the batter into a greased and floured loaf pan. Bake 60 to 70 minutes or until a toothpick inserted in the middle comes out clean. Check the cake at 25 minutes. If the cake is getting too brown, cover loosely with a piece of foil or parchment.

2 sticks unsalted butter
($1/2$ pound or 1 cup), softened
$1^{1}/_{2}$ cups sugar
$1^{1}/_{2}$ teaspoons vanilla extract
6 eggs
1 cup sour cream
4 tablespoons Hershey's European Dark Cocoa
$2^{1}/_{4}$ cups cake flour
$1/_{2}$ teaspoon baking powder
$1/_{4}$ teaspoon salt
$1/_{4}$ cup boiling water

Cool in the pan for 10 minutes. Loosen the sides with a metal spatula and invert onto a greased metal rack.

Serve plain, or with ice cream and a drizzle of hot fudge sauce, or frost with your favorite chocolate frosting.

Cook's Tips: Hershey's European Dark Cocoa is available at some supermarkets. Another excellent dark cocoa is made by Scharffen Berger and it can be found at Whole Foods and specialty kitchen stores. If you can't find either one, use regular baking cocoa.

This cake forms a dome in the middle of the loaf pan while baking (but should not spill over). When removing the cake from the pan, turn it over so that the smooth side is on top and slice as you would any pound cake. If the dome is too high or unattractive, you can slice the dome off to even it up and then turn it over. Serve with ice cream, or frost the cake, if desired, although it's tasty, as is.

Chocolate Cake with Warm Chocolate Sauce

This is a very dense, very delicious cake, similar to a flourless chocolate torte. You can serve it with the Warm Chocolate Sauce featured here, or you could cover it with the same ganache that is used over the White Chocolate Mousse recipe (see page 212).

MAKES 1 9-INCH CAKE ROUND

Preheat oven to 350 degrees.

Melt the chocolate, butter, and the whiskey in a double boiler. Cool to room temperature.

Combine egg yolks and $^1/_2$ cup sugar plus 3 tablespoons sugar (remove from the $1^1/_4$ cups sugar) in the bowl of an electric mixer. Beat on high until mixture reaches stage where batter is ribbonlike. In a separate bowl, mix together flour and salt. Fold flour into egg yolk mixture. Add cooled chocolate mixture and stir to combine. Pour into another bowl.

In the clean bowl of an electric mixer, whip egg whites until frothy. Add remaining sugar and whip to stiff peaks (about the consistency of meringue). Gently fold egg whites into chocolate mixture.

6 ounces bittersweet (not unsweetened) or semisweet chocolate
$^3/_4$ stick butter (3 ounces or 6 tablespoons)
$3^1/_3$ ounces whiskey
4 eggs, yolks and whites separated
$1^1/_4$ cups sugar, divided
1 cup flour
Pinch salt
Chocolate Sauce (see recipe that follows)

Grease sides and bottom of a 9-inch springform pan. Place a piece of parchment paper, cut to fit, into the bottom of the pan. Spray with aerosol cooking spray (such as Pam). Pour in cake batter.

Bake cake for 45 to 50 minutes. Do not overbake or cake will be dry. Cool for about 8 minutes.

Release sides of springform pan to free cake (if difficult to do, run a small knife around the sides to loosen). Turn over on plate and pull off parchment paper. Sprinkle cake with powdered sugar when cool. Serve with Warm Chocolate Sauce around cake slices. Alternatively, pour chocolate sauce over top of cake. (Sauce will harden when cool.)

Warm Chocolate Sauce

MAKES ³/₄ CUP

Melt chocolate with water over low heat. Remove from heat. Add butter and stir until melted.

¹/₂ pound bittersweet (not unsweetened) or semisweet chocolate
¹/₂ cup water
3 ounces butter

White Chocolate Mousse with Ganache

The ever-wonderful restaurateur Noel Cunningham of Strings gave us this recipe from chef Amy Vitale. White chocolate mousse with a layer of chocolate ganache over it? How could this be anything but fabulous.

SERVES 8

To make the mousse: Put white chocolate chips into the top of a double boiler, which is placed over the water-filled bottom half of the boiler. Heat chocolate just until pieces are melted; do not overheat. While chocolate is melting, whisk the gelatin into the 3 tablespoons of water.

Take melted chocolate off double boiler and whisk the gelatin/water mixture into the chocolate. Next, whisk in the pasteurized eggs.

In a separate bowl, whip $1^1/2$ cups of cream until stiff and fold it into the chocolate mixture. Pour mousse mixture into a mold (such as a gelatin mold or similar) and chill in refrigerator until firm.

To make the ganache: Chop the bittersweet chocolate into small pieces and place in a medium bowl. Bring the remaining 1 cup cream to a boil and pour it over the chopped choco-

12 ounces white chocolate chips
   (or chop up bars of white chocolate)
$1^1/2$ teaspoons powdered gelatin
3 tablespoons water
$^3/4$ cup pasteurized egg product,
   such as ReddiEgg
$2^1/2$ cups whipping cream, divided
8 ounces bittersweet (not unsweetened)
   chocolate
Fresh berries for garnish (optional)

late. Whisk until all chocolate pieces dissolve. Allow mixture to cool to room temperature.

To assemble: Loosen the mousse by holding onto the mold and running hot tap water over the sides and bottom for several seconds or dip the bottom briefly in hot water as for gelatin. Mousse will melt quickly, so don't dip too long. Carefully turn mousse out onto a plate and pour slightly warm ganache over it.

Decorate with fresh berries.

Cook's Tip: Use a fancy mold for the mousse, or put it in individual custard cups, or improvise— I used an oval-shaped stainless-steel bowl.

Chocolate Soup with Grand Marnier Flan

Okay, even we were intrigued with the name of this one—but, as it turns out, Chocolate Soup is actually a sauce for the Grand Marnier Flan.

SERVES 8

Preheat oven to 300 degrees.

In oven, heat 1 inch of water in a pan (water bath) large enough to hold 8 ramekins.

To prepare flan: Heat the half-and-half in a saucepan until it's warm to the touch; do not boil. Mix sugar, eggs, and Grand Marnier in a large bowl.

Strain warmed half-and-half through a sieve over the bowl of flan mixture. Stir well and ladle into the 8 ramekins, filling each halfway. Place in preheated water bath and bake for 60 to 70 minutes until firm.

To prepare soup: Shave both chocolates into a medium bowl and set aside. Bring heavy cream to a boil in a saucepan; turn off heat. Add the shaved chocolate. Stir in the Godiva liqueur. Continue stirring until chocolate is melted. Strain mixture through a sieve.

To serve: Gently spoon flan out of each ramekin and place in individual soup bowls. Pour the

> 2 cups half-and-half
> 1/2 cup plus 2 tablespoons sugar
> 7 eggs
> 1 tablespoon Grand Marnier
> 8 ounces semisweet baking chocolate
>   (preferably dark chocolate from
>   Burgundy)
> 2 ounces Gianduja chocolate
> 3 ounces Godiva chocolate liqueur
> 1 quart heavy cream
> Fresh fruit of your choice for garnish:
>   berries, bananas, melon

chocolate soup around the flan. Garnish with fresh fruit.

Cook's Tips: Gianduja chocolate (pronounced "jon-DOO-jah," is a hazelnut-chocolate confection that comes in 1-ounce pieces, available at specialty food stores.

The recipe for the soup can be halved easily, although you'll want to use these proportions: 1 pint heavy cream, 4 ounces dark semisweet chocolate, and 2 ounces (stays the same) hazelnut chocolate and 1 1/2 ounces (a jigger) of Godiva liqueur. The other option is to use the "chocolate soup" over ice cream.

Desserts

Vanilla Crème Brûlée with Fresh Raspberries

Crème brûlée is a baked custard dessert that has a glaze of sugar browned over the top. When you dip your spoon through the crackle of the hardened sugar to the custard beneath, you get both creamy and smooth textures.

SERVES 6

Preheat oven to 325 degrees.

In six $^3/_4$-cup ramekins, place raspberries on their sides in each dish—enough to cover the bottoms of the ramekins. Use remaining raspberries for garnish.

In a medium mixing bowl, whisk the yolks and the $^1/_2$ cup of sugar to blend. Into this mixture, scrape the seeds from inside the vanilla bean. Gradually whisk in the cream. Ladle mixture into each ramekin. Arrange ramekins in a 9 × 13-inch baking pan and add enough hot water to the pan to come halfway up sides of ramekins. Loosely cover the pan with foil and bake the custards until just set but still trembling slightly, about 60 minutes (but check at 45 minutes).

Carefully remove ramekins from the pan and cool on a rack. Chill custards in fridge, loosely

> 3 1-pint baskets fresh raspberries
> 6 large egg yolks
> Scant $^1/_2$ cup granulated sugar
> 1 vanilla bean, split lengthwise
> 2 cups heavy whipping cream
> 3 tablespoons turbinado (raw) sugar

covered with plastic wrap, until firm—at least 2 hours but not more than a day. Position oven rack so that tops of custards will be 2 to 3 inches from the broiler, and preheat broiler.

Sprinkle raw sugar evenly on top of each custard and caramelize under the hot broiler until sugar is melted and a deep golden brown.

Garnish with fresh raspberries and serve.

Cook's Tip: Turbinado, or raw sugar, available at grocery stores, is recommended for topping the crème brûlée, but you could substitute brown sugar. Cook custards until just set or they'll be watery.

You can also brown the sugar on top of the custards by using a handheld small chef's torch, sold at gourmet kitchenware stores.

Tiramisù

Although this recipe originally called for 36 ladyfingers and served 4, there was twice as much filling as needed, and cutting it further would have been difficult. Hence, we've opted to increase the number of ladyfingers and the Kahlua mixture, which will make enough for one layered 9 × 13-inch baking dish and will serve about 10—making it the perfect size for a dinner party dessert.

MAKES 1 9×13-INCH PAN

Shave chocolate using cheese grater.

In a large mixing bowl, combine mascarpone, sugar, and egg yolks and whisk until creamy.

In a small mixing bowl, beat egg whites to soft peaks.

Fold the two mixtures together, add the chocolate shavings, and blend with rubber spatula for 2 minutes. Combine half the Kahlua, half the rum, and half the espresso together in a shallow bowl wide enough for dipping the ladyfingers: Dip each one to coat on all sides, but do not soak.

In a shallow 9 × 13-inch glass baking dish, place ladyfingers face down to cover bottom

> 2 1-ounce squares of semisweet dark chocolate
> 2½ pounds mascarpone
> ½ cup sugar
> ⅓ cup egg yolks
> ⅓ cup egg whites
> 1 cup Kahlua
> 1 cup espresso (use instant espresso, prepared according to label directions)
> 1 cup rum
> 4 3-ounce packages of ladyfingers (about 48)

of pan. Spread the filling mixture over ladyfingers. Repeat twice, ending with ladyfingers on the top.

Cover baking pan with foil and refrigerate for at least 2 hours. Serve.

Cook's Tips: Because of the risk of salmonella with raw eggs, we used egg substitutes: Egg Beaters for the yolks and pasteurized whites that can be whipped, which are available at specialty stores.

Mascarpone is pricey, so you might try subbing sweetened whipped cream cheese for part of it.

Sticky Toffee Pudding Cake

Sticky toffee puddings are becoming increasingly popular and are being featured in magazines and cookbooks. Executive chef Bruce Yim and pastry chef Charles Broschinsky of the popular Sweet Basil restaurant came up with their version of the dessert, which is first-rate—just what you would expect from such an excellent restaurant.

MAKES 16 INDIVIDUAL
MUFFIN-SIZE PUDDINGS

Cover the dates with water and bring to a boil. Cook for 2 or 3 minutes. Remove and strain. When they have cooled enough to handle, peel and chop them. Return to the pan and cover with the 2 cups of water. Bring back to a boil, then remove from heat and set aside.

Preheat oven to 325 degrees.

When the dates have cooled a bit—do not drain—stir in the baking soda and vanilla. In a small bowl, sift the baking powder, flour, and salt together. In the mixing bowl of an electric mixer, cream the butter and the sugar together, then add the eggs. Stir in part of the dates with their liquid, then part of the dry ingredients.

2^1/$_4$ cups pitted dates
2 cups water
2 teaspoons baking soda
2 teaspoons vanilla extract
1 teaspoon baking powder
4 cups all-purpose flour
1 teaspoon salt
1 stick butter (^{1}/$_4$ pound or ^{1}/$_2$ cup), softened
1^1/$_2$ cups sugar
2 eggs
Toffee Sauce (see recipe that follows)

Alternate dry and wet ingredients until all ingredients are in the mixer and the batter is smooth. Fill greased muffin tins no more than three-fourths full.

Spray a piece of parchment paper with cooking spray and cover tins with the parchment paper, greased side down. Cover parchment paper with a cookie sheet. The cookie sheet keeps the batter in the muffin tins from rising too high (and thus keeps them dense and compact).

Bake for approximately 15 to 20 minutes. When slightly browned and firm, remove from oven. Let cool and remove the puddings from the tins. Next, fill the muffin tins or individual ramekins about one-fourth full with Toffee Sauce, then return the puddings to the tins or to ramekins. You may serve right away or refrigerate until serving time. Before serving, remove puddings from the tin and warm in the microwave oven for 1 minute with some additional sauce. Top with soft whipped cream.

Toffee Sauce

MAKES ABOUT 10 PORTIONS

Melt the butter and sugar together in a $1^{1}/_{2}$- to 2-quart saucepan. Stir in the cream and bring to a full boil. (Use a pan large enough to allow for the sauce to boil up.) Remove from heat and let cool a bit before stirring in the liquor.

Cook's Tip: Do not use chopped dates with added sugar (check the package).

1 stick butter ($^{1}/_{4}$ pound or $^{1}/_{2}$ cup)
2 cups brown sugar
2 cups heavy cream
2 tablespoons dark rum or brandy

Bread Pudding with Caramel Sauce

This lovely restaurant is known for its gardens and its food. If you want to simplify this recipe, use a jar of high-quality caramel sauce instead of making your own caramel.

SERVES 8

Preheat oven to 350 degrees.

Line the bottom and sides of a 9-inch springform pan with buttered parchment paper. Whisk together eggs, milk, 1/2 cup sugar, vanilla, cinnamon, nutmeg, and salt.

Soak bread briefly in egg mixture and layer it in the springform pan. (This is the time to sprinkle in any optional add-ins.)

Cut together all butter, flour, 1/4 cup sugar, and brown sugar until mixture looks like coarse cornmeal. Sprinkle topping over the bread mixture. Prepare a water bath: Place springform pan inside a larger pan, and add hot water to the outside pan until water reaches halfway up the side of the springform pan. Bake for an hour to an hour and 15 minutes, or until golden brown.

While the pudding bakes, prepare caramel sauce.

3 eggs
3 cups milk or half-and-half
3/4 cup sugar, divided
1 teaspoon vanilla extract
1 teaspoon cinnamon
1 teaspoon nutmeg
1/2 teaspoon salt (optional)
1 loaf day-old french bread,
    sliced 1/2-inch thick
Optional add-ins: walnuts,
    raisins, blueberries,
    dried apricots cut into quarters
1 1/2 sticks butter, cut into small pieces
1/2 cup flour
1/4 cup brown sugar
Caramel Sauce (see recipe that follows)

Remove springform pan from water bath and let cool. Invert cooled pudding onto a plate and remove parchment paper. Then invert again onto a serving platter so topping is on top. Serve with caramel sauce. (Leftover sauce can be used on ice cream.)

Caramel Sauce

MAKES 3 CUPS

Stir sugar and 1$^1/_2$ cups cream in a saucepan on medium heat until sugar dissolves. Turn up heat and continue to cook at a boil, holding the pot handle and swirling mixture over heat until mixture turns golden brown. Be very careful, mixture will bubble up and is very hot.

2 cups sugar
2 cups heavy cream

Watch carefully to avoid burning—mixture will thicken more as it cools. Remove from heat, fold in the remaining $^1/_2$ cup cream and stir. (Be careful again; mixture will bubble up and is very hot.) Mix until sauce is smooth.

• •

Jack Daniels Bread Pudding

Croissants? Caramel sauce? Jack Daniels? This pudding was even good served cold the next day.

MAKES 6 SERVINGS

Preheat oven to 350 degrees.

In a saucepan, bring the cream, sugar, and vanilla to a boil. Then remove from heat and slowly stir a third of the mix into the egg yolks. Add yolk mixture to remaining cream-sugar mix. Divide and spoon the caramel sauce into buttered 8-ounce custard or soufflé cups, and set aside.

Dice the croissants into medium-sized pieces and place in a large bowl. Pour the cream mix and Jack Daniels over the croissants, and let them soak for 15 minutes. Scoop this mixture into the prepared cups and bake covered in a water bath in the oven for 30 minutes or until firm.

Let it cool for 20 minutes. Turn the bread pudding out of the cups onto plates: Hot caramel sauce should drip down the sides of the pudding. Top with walnuts.

$2^1/_4$ cups cream
$^1/_2$ cup sugar
1 tablespoon vanilla extract
7 egg yolks, lightly beaten
$^1/_4$ cup caramel sauce
   (store-bought ice cream topping)
5 large croissants
3 tablespoons Jack Daniels
$^1/_2$ cup chopped walnuts for topping

Cook's Tip: *A water bath is used to cook delicate foods gently. To create a water bath, place the custard cups in a larger pan, such as a 9 × 13-inch size, and pour hot water into the pan, so that the water rises at least halfway up the sides of the custard cups.*

• •

Tres Leches Bread Pudding

This dish was part of a specialty menu created by executive chef Paul Wade, who was featuring dishes from other countries. His tres leches— or "three milk"—bread pudding is a delicious Mexican variation on a theme.

MAKES 1 9 × 13-INCH PAN

Combine three milks, eggs, cinnamon, and 1 teaspoon sugar and mix well. Combine bread cubes and custard. Allow to rest 1 hour.

Preheat oven to 325 degrees.

Bake bread-and-custard mixture in 6 to 8 oven-proof ramekins or in a 9 × 13-inch baking dish in a water bath (i.e., in a larger pan with water that comes halfway up the sides of the dish). Cover with foil halfway through cooking— total cooking time is 1 hour and 15 minutes (check at 1 hour) or until firm and custard is cooked.

Allow to rest 20 minutes. Meanwhile, prepare bananas: Mix remaining $1/4$ cup of sugar and melted butter in a saucepan. Cook until light brown. Remove from heat. Add bananas to pan, mixing with butter and sugar.

2 cups sweetened condensed milk
2 cups coconut milk
4 tablespoons whole milk
2 eggs
$3/4$ teaspoon ground cinnamon
$1/4$ cup plus 1 teaspoon sugar, divided
1 pound brioche, cut into 1-inch by 1-inch cubes (if you can't find brioche, substitute Challah egg bread or packaged sweet yeast rolls)
2 bananas, peeled, sliced in half lengthwise and then in half crosswise
4 tablespoons melted butter

Serve bread pudding with your favorite ice cream and the caramelized bananas.

Bread Pudding with Vanilla Sauce

MAKES 1 9 × 13-INCH PAN

Preheat oven to 300 degrees.

Coat a 9 × 13-inch pan with cooking spray. Mix the nutmeg and cinnamon with the sugar to avoid lumps. Beat eggs, sugar mixture, and vanilla. Add the milk and mix thoroughly. Pour half of the raisins on bottom of pan, then add bread and top with rest of raisins. Ladle the egg mixture over bread. Cook for about an hour. Cover tightly with foil and bake another half hour or until custard is set. Serve with Vanilla Sauce.

1 teaspoon nutmeg
1 teaspoon cinnamon
1 scant cup sugar
8 eggs
1/2 teaspoon vanilla extract
1 quart milk
1/2 to 1 cup of raisins,
    depending on preference
1/2 loaf French bread torn into 1-inch pieces
Vanilla Sauce (see recipe that follows)

Vanilla Sauce

MAKES 2 CUPS

Heat milk, cream, 1 tablespoon sugar, 7 tablespoons half-and-half, and vanilla bean in top of a double boiler. Mix 1 teaspoon sugar, cornstarch, egg yolks, and 2 tablespoons half-and-half in a mixer. Add egg mixture back to the remaining milk mixture still in the double boiler. Continue to cook over double boiler, whisking throughout, until mixture coats the back of a spoon. Strain and cool in refrigerator.

3/4 cup milk
1/2 cup heavy cream
1 tablespoon plus 1 teaspoon sugar, divided
9 tablespoons half-and-half, divided
1 vanilla bean
1 teaspoon cornstarch
3 egg yolks

Bread Pudding with Ice Cream Crème Anglaise

Both Trinity Grille and Castle Café serve this bread pudding. The recipe is unusual in that it has honey in the mixture. Crème Anglaise is a creamy custard sauce, which could be a dessert by itself if served over fruit. Interestingly, this one adds ice cream to the custard sauce.

MAKES 1 9 × 13-INCH PAN

Preheat oven to 350 degrees.

Bring milk and 2 cups cream almost to a boil. Remove from burner and toss dinner rolls in mixture. Set aside.

In a large bowl, whisk together sugar, honey, eggs and yolks, cinnamon, nutmeg, butter, and vanilla. Pour over rolls and cream in a lightly greased 9 × 13-inch pan. Put bread pudding pan into larger pan filled with $1/2$-inch hot water for water bath. Bake in oven for 45 minutes. Allow to cool.

Pour $1/2$ cup cream evenly over top of pudding and coat liberally with sugar and cinnamon. Place bread pudding under broiler only until brown (watch closely — do not burn).

4 cups milk
2 cups cream
1 dozen (about a pound) dinner rolls, cut in $3/4$-inch dice
1 cup sugar
$1/4$ cup honey
4 eggs plus 2 egg yolks
2 teaspoons cinnamon
$1/2$ teaspoon nutmeg
4 ounces butter, melted
$11/2$ tablespoons vanilla extract
$1/2$ cup additional cream, sugar, and cinnamon for topping
Crème Anglaise (see recipe that follows)

Cut pudding into squares to serve and pour warm Crème Anglaise into each dish of pudding, surrounding the pudding.

(continued on next page)

Crème Anglaise

Bring milk to boil over medium heat, then remove from burner. Scrape the seeds from the vanilla beans and add with the hulls to the milk.

Whisk together the sugar and cornstarch. Add salt and eggs and whisk until smooth.

Add a small portion of hot milk to temper the eggs and whisk; return to milk in pot and cook until thickened, stirring constantly. Add ice cream and stir until melted and combined.

Strain sauce.

5 cups milk
2 vanilla beans, split in half lengthwise
1 cup sugar
$1/4$ cup cornstarch
Pinch of salt
3 eggs
1 pint vanilla ice cream

Pumpkin Bread Pudding

Omigosh! This bread pudding combines brownies, canned pumpkin, and custard. A sweet trifecta!

MAKES 1 9 × 13-INCH PAN

Preheat oven to 350 degrees.

Toss bread with melted butter. Bake in pan for 15 minutes, then cool.

Whisk together half-and-half, sugar, eggs, vanilla, and cinnamon.

Mixture will just fit into a 9 × 13-inch pan. Layer cooled bread, pumpkin, brownies, canned pumpkin, and white chocolate chips. Pour custard over all. Let rest for 15 minutes. Place in refrigerator for 2 hours or overnight, covered with foil.

Bake bread pudding at 325 degrees in a water bath (place bread pudding pan in a larger pan of warm water so that water comes halfway up the sides of the bread pudding pan) for $1^1/2$ hours. Let cool; cut.

1 pound challah or brioche,
   cut into 1-inch cubes
$^1/2$ stick butter, melted
1 quart half-and-half
$1^1/2$ cups finely granulated sugar
10 eggs
1 tablespoon vanilla
$^1/2$ tablespoon cinnamon
1 pound canned pumpkin
$^1/2$ pound chocolate brownies,
   cut into $^1/2$-inch pieces
2 cups white chocolate chips

Cook's Tip: Make or buy the brownies before you begin. Also, if you want to use a smaller, deeper pan, double the layers.

Pearl Street Grill Bread Pudding

This recipe differs from some of the others in this book in that it uses sourdough bread. But as with the other versions, it's comfort food at its finest.

MAKES 1 9 × 13-INCH PAN

Preheat oven to 350 degrees.

Tear bread into bite-sized pieces and place in a 9 × 13-inch pan.

In a bowl whisk together the eggs, half-and-half, vanilla, sugar, and the orange juice. Add the cinnamon and the raisins.

Drizzle the melted butter over the bread. Pour the egg mixture over the bread and allow to soak for 20 minutes.

Cover the pan with foil and bake in a water bath. (Place 9 × 13-inch pan in a larger pan. Pour hot

> 3/4 pound sourdough bread, sliced
> 5 eggs
> 1 1/4 quarts half-and-half
> 1 1/2 tablespoons vanilla
> 3/4 cup sugar
> 1/2 cup orange juice
> 1 tablespoon cinnamon
> 3/4 cup raisins
> 1/2 cup melted butter
> Pudding Sauce (see recipe that follows)

water in larger pan to come at least halfway up sides of smaller pan.) Bake 30 minutes covered with foil; uncover and continue to bake another 30 minutes or until custard is set. Let pudding cool. Serve warm with Pudding Sauce.

Cook's Tip: *A water bath is used to cook the custard gently and avoid curdling.*

Pudding Sauce

> 1/2 stick butter, softened
> 1 cup brown sugar
> 1 cup half-and-half
> 1/4 cup brandy
> 1 teaspoon vanilla

MAKES 1 1/2 CUPS

Cream together butter and sugar in a bowl. Heat butter mixture in a saucepan with the half-and-half. Stir constantly until smooth. Remove from heat. Add brandy and vanilla. Stir and serve warm.

The Restaurants

Note: Restaurants change locations and phone numbers regularly, so be sure to check information to make sure it's current. Restaurants without addresses are no longer in business.

Adams Mountain Café
110 Canyon Ave.
Manitou Springs, CO 80829
719-685-1430

Aubergine
    (Chef/Owner Sean Kelly now
    owns Clair de Lune located at
    1313 E. 6th Ave., Denver, CO
    80218, 303-831-1992)

Augustine Grill
519 Wilcox St.
Castle Rock, CO 80104
303-814-3663

Aurora Summit Steak House
2700 S. Havana St.
Aurora, CO 80014
303-751-2112

Avenue Grill
630 E. 17th Ave.
Denver, CO 80203
303-861-2820

Bambino's
1135 Bannock
Denver, CO 80204
303-221-7215

Bang!
3472 W. 32nd Ave.
Denver, CO 80211

Bella Ristorante

Big Ray's Chop House
10188 U.S. 34
(Between Granby and
    Grand Lake), CO
970-627-9300

Black-Eyed Pea (numerous
    metro Denver locations)
1470 S. Colorado Blvd.
Denver, CO 80222
303-691-3470

Bluepoint Bakery, wholesale only
    (for Pour La France)
1721 E. 58th Ave.
Denver, CO 80216
303-298-1100

Bravo! Ristorante
    at the Adams Mark
1500 Court Place
Denver, CO 80202
303-626-2581

Briarwood Inn
1630 8th St.
Golden, CO 80401
303-279-3121

Broadmoor Hotel, Charles Court
1 Lake Ave.
Colorado Springs, CO 80906
719-634-7711

The Broker (Downtown)
821 17th St.
Denver, CO 80202
303-292-5065
The Broker (Boulder Inn)
555 30th St.
Boulder, CO 80303
303-449-1752

Brown Palace (Ellyington's,
    Palace Arms, Ship's Tavern)
321 17th St.
Denver, CO. 80202
303-297-3111

Bruno's Italian Bistro
2223 S. Monaco Pkwy.
Denver, CO 80222
303-757-4500

Bull and Bush
(also Marina Landing)
4700 Cherry Creek S. Drive
Glendale, CO 80246
303-759-0333

Bump & Grind
439 E. 17th Ave.
Denver, CO 80203
303-861-4841

Cadillac Ranch

Café Giovanni

Café Gondolier
1738 Pearl St.
Boulder, CO 80302

California Café
8505 Park Meadows Center Drive
(in Park Meadows Mall)
Littleton, CO 80124
303-649-1111

Carmine's on Penn
92 S. Pennsylvania St.
Denver, CO 80209
303-777-6443

Castle Café
403 Wilcox St.
Castle Rock, CO 80104
303-814-2233

Chautauqua Dining Hall
900 Baseline Rd.
Boulder, CO 80302
303-440-3776

Cherry Hills Country Club
4125 S. University Blvd.
Cherry Hills Village, CO 80110
303-761-9900.

Chinook Tavern
265 Detroit St.
Denver, CO 80206
303-394-0044

Chives

Chopper's Sports Grill
80 S. Madison
Denver, CO 80209
303-329-0995

Cool River Café
8000 E. Belleview Ave.
Greenwood Village, CO 80111
303-771-4117

Dazzle
930 Lincoln St.
Denver, CO 80203
303-839-5100

Denver Buffalo Company

Dixons Downtown Grill
1610 16th St.
Denver, CO 80202
303-573-6100

El Rancho
29260 U.S. Highway 40
Golden, CO 80401
303-526-0661

Epicurean Catering
6022 S. Holly St.
Greenwood Village, CO 80111
303-770-0877

The Fort
19192 Highway 8
Morrison, CO 80465
303-697-4771

Hacienda Colorado
10500 Bierstadt Way
Englewood, CO 80112
303-858-8588

Hearthstone
130 S. Ridge St.
Breckenridge, CO 80424

Highland's Garden Café
3927 W. 32nd Ave.
Denver, CO 80212
303-458-5920

Imperial Chinese Seafood
431 S. Broadway
Denver, CO 80209
303-698-2800

Jax Fish House
1539 17th St.
Denver, CO 80202
303-292-5767

The Restaurants

Jay's American Bistro
135 W. Oak St.
Ft. Collins, CO 80524
970-482-1876

Josephina's
1433 Larimer St.
Denver, CO 80202
303-623-0166

Karen's in the Country
1900 Plaza Dr.
Louisville, CO 80027
303-666-8503

Kevin Taylor Restaurant
   (Hotel Teatro)
1106 14th St.
Denver, CO 80202
303-820-2600

Luigi's Bent Noodle
3055 S. Parker Rd.
Aurora, CO 80014
303-337-2733
(Second location)
8130 S. University Blvd.
Littleton, CO 80122
303-694-9357

Maggiano's Little Italy
500 16th St.
   (in the Denver Pavilions)
Denver, CO 80202
303-260-7707
(Second location)
7401 S. Clinton St.
Englewood, CO 80112
303-858-1405

The Market
1445 Larimer St.
Denver, CO 80202
303-534-5140

McCormick's Fish House and Bar
   (in the Oxford Hotel)
1659 Wazee St.
Denver, CO 80202
303-825-1107

Mel's Restaurant and Bar
235 Fillmore St.
Denver, CO 80206
303-333-3979

Mexicali Cafe

Montagna
   (in the Little Nell Hotel)
675 E. Durant Ave.
Aspen, CO 81611
970-920-6313

Morton's of Chicago
1710 Wynkoop St.
Denver, CO 80202
303-825-3353
(Second location)
8480 E. Belleview Ave.
Greenwood Village, CO 80111
303-409-1177

New Orient
10203 E. Iliff Ave.
Denver, CO 80213
303-751-1288

Normandy

Old Neighborhood Restaurant
7923 Allison Way
Arvada, CO 80005
303-425-1962

O's Steak and Seafood
   (in the Westminster Westin Hotel)
10600 Westminster Blvd.
Westminster, CO 80030
303-410-5060

Palace Chinese
6265 E. Evans Ave.
Denver, CO 80222
303-782-0300

Palettes (Denver Art Museum)
100 W. 14th Ave. Parkway
Denver, CO 80204
303-629-0889

Palmetto Grille
(Chef/owner Michael Bortz is now corporate baker for Paradise Bakery at 105 E. Seventh Ave. (303-832-6300).

Panzano
909 17th St.
Denver, CO 80202
303-296-3535

Pasta Pasta Pasta
278 Fillmore St.
Denver, CO 80206
303-377-2782

Pasta's
9126 W. Bowles Ave.
Littleton, CO 80123
303-933-2829

Paul's Catering
www.paulscateringdenver.com
303-781-8335

Pearl Street Grill
1477 S. Pearl St.
Denver, CO 80215
303-778-6475

Pesce Fresco
6600 S. Quebec St.
Centennial, CO 80111
303-290-9705

Pomodoro

Racines
650 Sherman St.
Denver, CO 80203
303-595-0418

Randolph's (in the Warwick Hotel)
1776 Grant
Denver, CO 80203
303-861-2000

Red Coral
1591 S. Colorado Blvd.
Denver, CO 80222
303-758-7610

Rocky Mountain Diner
800 18th St.
Denver, CO 80202
303-293-8383

Sage Southwestern Grill
323 14th St.
Denver, CO 80202
303-797-2181

Sansone's Chez Walter
5969 S. University Blvd.
Greenwood Village, CO 80121
303-794-4026

Seven 30 South
730 S. University Blvd.
Denver, CO 80209
303-744-1888

Silverheels at the Ore House
601 Main Street
Frisco, Colorado 80443
970-668-0345

Steamworks Brewing Company
801 E. Second Ave.
Durango, CO
Toll-free (877) 372-9200,

Strings
1700 Humboldt St.
Denver, CO 80218
303-831-7310

Sweet Basil
193 E. Gore Creek Dr.
Vail, CO 81657
970-476-0125

Sweet Rockin' Coffee
414 E. 20th Ave.
Denver, CO 80205
303-318-9788

Trinity Grille
1801 Broadway
Denver, CO 80202
303-293-2288

Turley's
2350 Arapahoe Ave.
Boulder, CO 80302
303-442-2800

240 Union
240 Union Blvd.
Lakewood, CO 80228
303-989-3562

Vesta Dipping Grill
1822 Blake St.
Denver, CO 80202
303-296-1970

Washington Park Grill
1096 S. Gaylord St.
Denver, CO 80209
303-777-0707

Watercourse Foods
206 E. 13th Ave.
Denver, CO 80203
303-832-7313

Wellshire Inn
3333 S. Colorado Blvd.
Denver, CO 80222
303-759-3333

Wolfgang Puck Grand Café
500 16th St.
  (2nd Floor, Denver Pavilions)
Denver, CO 80202
303-595-9653

Wynkoop Brewing Company
1634 18th St.
Denver, CO 80202
303-297-2700

Zenith

Index

Index

❧ *237* ❧

Index

Index

Index

❧ *244* ❧

Index

Index